EVERYONE'S PROBLEM SOLVING

SOLVING

HANDBOOK

EVERYONE'S PROBLEM SOLVING

SOLVING

HANDBOOK

Step-by-Step Solutions for Quality Improvement

Michael R. Kelly

Productivity Press | Portland, Oregon

Productivity Press
P.O. Box 13390
Portland, Oregon 97213-0390
United States of America
Telephone: 503-235-0600
Telefax: 503-235-0909
E-mail: info@productivityinc.com

Printed in the United States of America

Library of Congress Cataloging-in-Publication Data

Kelly, Michael R.
    Everyone's problem-solving handbook / Michael R. Kelly.
       p. cm.
    Includes bibliographical references and index.
    ISBN 0-527-91652-8 (alk. paper)
    1. Problem solving. I. Title.
HD30.29.K45 1992
658.4'03—dc20

91-40137
CIP

05 04 03   10 9 8 7

CONTENTS

Preface . . . . vii-ix

Chapter One: A New Way of Thinking 1-15

Chapter Two: A Systematic Approach 17-45

    Step 1: Identify the Problem 23
    Step 2: Analyze 29
    Step 3: Evaluate Alternatives 34
    Step 4: Test-Implement 40
    Step 5: Standardize 42

Chapter Three: Tools for Quality Improvement 47-105

    Bar Chart 49
    Barriers & Aids 53
    Brainstorming 56
    Cause-and-Effect Diagram 59
    Checksheet 66
    Flowchart 69
    Histogram 72
    Interview 79
    Line Graph 82
    List Reduction 85
    Matrix 87
    Pareto Chart 92
    Pie Chart 98
    Survey 102

Chapter Four:
Applying the Tools for Quality Improvement 107-153

    Case 1: Measuring Training Effectiveness 109
    Case 2: Suggestions Anyone? 117
    Case 3: Handling Customer Inquiries 123
    Case 4: Processing Invoices for Payment 131
    Case 5: Improving Employee Safety 138
    The QI Story 147

Glossary 155-156

Bibliography 157

Index 159-165

PREFACE

This book is for the person with the skills to do his or her work, and who tries to do the best job possible, but often is unable to influence others to make changes when they are needed.

If this describes a frustration you sometimes feel on the job, you are not alone. Many employees are frustrated because of their inability to influence the system in which they operate. When you are not able to do your best, whatever the cause, the result is products and services that are not at a level where they could and should be—quality is not built in.

Not many people are satisfied with a situation that does not allow their voice to be heard. When you can't influence others to make needed changes, how can you be happy with a product that you know is less than satisfactory? Pride in craftsmanship is eliminated, and staying away from work becomes a plausible alternative. After all, why work when work makes you unhappy? Well, yes, there is the money. But money only brings temporary relief from a day-to-day situation where you are not paid to think. Staying away from work under these circumstances doesn't mean that you don't want to work, rather, it means you are frustrated because you have not been given the opportunity to do your best.

In this book I want to help you understand that by using some simple work tools, and a set of problem-solving steps, you can make a difference in the way you approach work and in the way you approach life. I want you to use them to improve your work, to improve the conditions in which you work, and to make better products that I would want to buy some day.

I first came in contact with the tools for quality improvement at Florida Power & Light Company (FPL). As employees at FPL, we were taught to apply these tools to our work. Looking back, I believe our objective was to make improvements that would benefit:

- the employees involved, by making the work easier,
- the company, through more efficient or effective work activities, and
- the customer(s) of our work, who had to use what we produced.

At FPL we learned to think in terms of the tools for quality improvement. This must sound foreign to you. Even writing it causes me to consider how far we came in our application of these basic quality concepts. What I mean by thinking in terms of the tools is that our daily work was merged with using and understanding them. We used the tools for quality improvement during formal presentations, regular meetings (management, staff, safety, etc.), and even during informal conversations to clarify a point. In fact we used them like conversation, because they are so useful for clearly communicating ideas. Dr. Hitoshi Kume, probably the world's foremost authority on the application of quality tools, refers to what we achieved as "a statistical way of thinking." In this book, because it sounds less threatening, I refer to this same concept as a "new way of thinking."

At FPL we often used the tools in association with a systematic approach to solving problems. You will be introduced to a similar problem-solving process in Chapter 2. Using these problem-solving steps with the tools for quality improvement, you will learn how you can make a meaningful contribution to your daily work.

In Chapter 3 the tools for quality improvement are listed in alphabetical order. This approach is used for easy reference. As to the selection of tools, I include only those that I believe you will use most often. There are other tools, of course. Most notable and useful is the control chart. This and other tools are not included because they require a deeper understanding of mathematics than I intended for this text. Referring back to Dr. Kume, he believes that 80% of the problems we face on the job can be corrected with just three tools: the checksheet, Pareto analysis, and cause-and-effect analysis. These three tools are included in this book, along with others that I'm confident will help you become more effective in your work.

Each tool is described using the same format. A *definition* is provided along with a brief description of how to *use* the tool. Immediately following is an *example* of what the tool looks like in its completed form. My intent is to provide you with an overall impression of whether or not a given tool can help meet your needs by looking at these three items. Once a tool has been identified as a potential work aid, you can follow the *step-by-step instructions* provided next. You will find that some of the tools are easier to use than others. But I believe the instructions are clear enough to enable you to apply any of the tools for quality improvement easily and correctly.

A final bit of information provided with each tool should be quite helpful in developing your understanding. The *helpful hints* are a voice of experience, accumulated from many, differing applications of the tools. They are offered to help you apply the tools correctly and to avoid making some of the mistakes others have made along the way.

Chapter 4 pulls together all that has been provided in the other chapters. There are five case studies that show what can be accomplished using the tools for quality improvement in association with the problem-solving steps. Reading these case studies should help solidify your understanding of the tools and lead you to start thinking differently about your work.

I hope you find this book to be a valuable reference. Using the tools will help you conserve resources and produce better products and services. The tools will help you prove to others that you are committed to, and capable of, making things better and improving quality. I'm confident that as you use the tools for quality improvement, you will find them easy to apply and even fun to use.

Many hours went into the preparation of this book. I'd like to thank those who contributed their time, talent, and wisdom. In particular I am indebted to Bill Cunningham, Sharon and Lisa Tuttle, and all the employees of Florida Power & Light Co., who endured, sacrificed, and were awarded the first Deming Overseas Prize.

One

A New Way of Thinking

The Gap

There is a gap between what we were taught in school and what we need to know. In some of us the gap is wider than in others. The size of the gap depends upon our background, experience, and education. This book addresses that part of the gap that originates from our education, and in particular, the dreaded subject of mathematics.

Have you ever wondered why so many people fear math? Maybe it's because we never clearly understood the books we were given. Remember your old math books? If you still have one, or if you can get your hands on the one your son or daughter brings home from school, pick it up and look through the pages. Still confusing isn't it? Most of these math books are just not user friendly. What I mean is that they are mathematically correct, but hard to follow. Most are written by men and women who have an excellent grasp of mathematics. In fact, the authors have more knowledge than I could hope to accumulate. But their math books do little to communicate to those of us who are less knowledgeable. We learners have been attempting to wade through these confusing books for years. Sometimes we are fortunate enough to have a good teacher explain what the authors meant, but in the absence of a good teacher, it's no wonder so many of us fear math.

Another reason I think we fear mathematics is that we don't clearly see how it can benefit us. Understanding mathematics takes a fair amount of concentration for the average person. This translates into an investment of time and effort. When the payoff for your investment is not made clear, it's a small wonder why the investment is never made.

Think about the problems that seem to find their way into almost every math book: *Johnny is traveling from Chicago to Los Angeles. His train left at 10 A.M. and is traveling at 60 MPH. The train is scheduled to make one stop for 45 minutes before arriving. If the distance from Chicago to Los Angeles is 1741 miles, when will Johnny's train arrive?*

Now, really, what incentive do you have for calculating this information? Aren't the train schedules published regularly? Certainly, there is a need to understand how to derive the answer, but my point is that questions like this don't provide a strong incentive to learn. We need to see clearly how the math we learn can help us cope with day-to-day life before we will be willing to invest the time and effort it takes to learn.

What Do We Need To Know?

There is another problem with the math skills we were taught in school. I don't believe they are sufficient to equip us for the problems we commonly face in the real world. In the world where I live and work, problems like Johnny's are a piece of cake. We face tougher problems like: *Johnny sent an invoice to the XYZ company on July 7. It is now August 22, and Johnny still hasn't received his check. Why is the check late? What is causing this problem? What can be done to keep the problem from recurring?*

The math tools most of us were taught in school won't help us solve this problem, or others like it. Yet, these are the kinds of problems that discourage us, because we are not equipped to solve them. We weren't given the tools we need to make the necessary improvements. Our tool kit is half empty. It's like trying to unscrew a phillips screw when all you have is a flat-head screwdriver.

Instead of being frustrated by these real world problems, we need to have knowledge of the tools required to solve them. The tools you will be introduced to in this book are provided with the needs of today's worker in mind. They can be easily understood and applied to help solve the problems you face daily; many examples are included to help with this. The tools are also presented in a format that will enable you to use this book as a reference while developing your skills in using them.

Beyond what has been provided in this book, I can't give you an incentive to learn the tools for quality improvement. Such inspiration has to come from within. What I can give you though is a quotation from a great American.

> *Hard work and best efforts, put forth without the guidance of knowledge, leads to ruin in the world that we are in today.*
>
> —*W. Edwards Deming*

W. Edwards Deming has lived his life sharing and searching for knowledge. He is the man who planted the seeds of change in Japan. By adopting Dr. Deming's philosophies and teachings the Japanese have improved the quality of their products and services from producing what was once considered junk to being respected as a worldwide leader in quality and value.

The opportunity seized by the Japanese is also available to us, but each of us must do our part to accept the challenge. It requires us to close the gap between what we know and what we need to know. We must increase our knowledge. My hope is that you will give yourself the opportunity to use the tools for quality improvement. Don't let past fears and doubts hold you back. Be open-minded and recognize that there is a better way if you are willing to accept it. Ask questions. Search for answers. Dr. Deming is the perfect example of what I mean. As of this writing he is 91 years young, still searching for knowledge, because he knows that a mind willing to challenge and question is a mind alive with potential.

What Are The Tools For Quality Improvement?

Figure 1-1 lists the tools for quality improvement that are covered in this text. The figure also suggests how the tools can help you. With the proper application of these simple tools you will be able to solve the vast majority of process-related problems you face both at home and in the workplace.

Knowledge Of A Process

Using the Tools for Quality Improvement effectively requires that you have some understanding of a process. *A process is the set of activities necessary to accomplish a task or produce an output.* There is a process involved in most everything we do. Driving a car involves a process that begins when we get in the car, insert a key in the ignition, and put the car in gear. In the kitchen there are processes, too. One that is easy to recognize is described in a recipe. Recipes include a set of activities necessary to produce something to eat. Recipes, driving a car, and the way you perform your work all involve processes—activities necessary to accomplish a task or produce an output.

In addition, it is important to understand that all processes have a set of influences (people, machinery, methods, materials) that combine to make each process output unique. This *variation* in output is the natural result of changes in the combination of influences that occur each time a process is performed. For example, the time it takes to get from point A to point B in a car is dependent on the driver (person), the car (machine), the driver's driving habits (methods), and maybe the octane of the gas the car is using (materials). In the kitchen, how good a recipe tastes is dependent on the cook (person), the kitchen appliances (machinery), the recipe itself (methods), and the ingredients (materials).

Variation in the output of a process is normal. Controlling the amount of variation, though, can lead to improvements in the quality of process outputs. Processes, and the variation that occurs naturally when they are executed, are what the tools for quality improvement can be used to influence.

TOOLS FOR QUALITY IMPROVEMENT	
TOOL	**THIS TOOL WILL HELP YOU**
Bar Chart	Arrange data for quick and easy comparison.
Barriers & Aids	Document the hindering and supporting factors that can or do influence a planned activity.
Brainstorming	Collect a large number of ideas from a group of people.
Cause-and-Effect Diagram	Identify a set of related causes that lead to an effect or problem.
Checksheet	Collect data in an organized manner.
Flowchart	Differentiate between the activities in a process.
Histogram	Determine how data are distributed.
Interview	Collect data from direct conversation.
Line Graph	Display the output of a process over time.
List Reduction	Reduce a large list of items to a manageable few.
Matrix	Make comparisons between two or more sets of information.
Pareto Chart	Arrange data so that the most significant element in a set of elements is easily identifiable.
Pie Chart	Display the volume or quantity of one item in relation to others.
Survey	Collect data from a large number of people.

Figure 1-1

An Example

Let's assume that you operate a car wash business. The owner informs you that during the coming year a 25 percent increase in cars washed is expected. Under normal circumstances this could cause you some pain, but you have applied the tools in this book and respond by saying that you can deliver 30 percent! The owner looks astonished as you continue by stating that this increase will require an up-front investment of $11,000 in advertising and equipment.

"What do you mean?" the owner asks, sounding interested.

You say that a *SURVEY** was used to identify the reasons customers choose one car wash over another. The survey findings have been summarized using a *PARETO CHART,* as shown in Figure 1-2.

You tell the owner that the survey indicates that the *quality* of your car wash is good, but you believe actions can be taken that will improve *cost* and *quick*

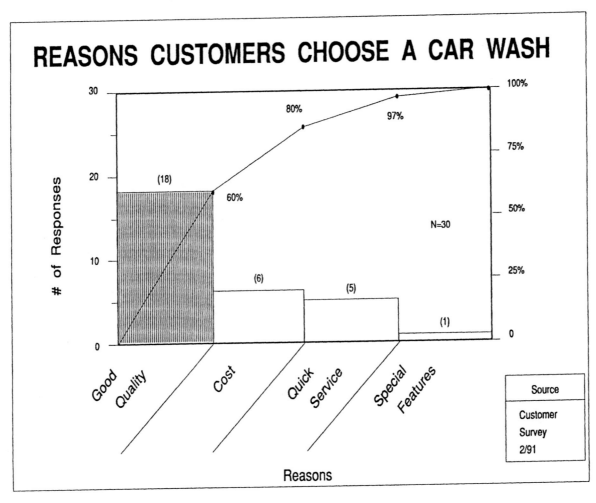

Figure 1-2. Pareto Chart

---

*   The tools for quality improvement are described more fully in Chapter 3.

service. You refer to some analysis that you have performed that has led you to believe that the number of cars washed can be increased if you do two things: advertise discounts and improve equipment efficiency.

Referring to the *PARETO CHART* in Figure 1-2, you explain to the owner that next to good quality, customers feel cost is most important.

You suggest advertising a discount (good through Saturday) in Wednesday's paper to attract more customers. The weekend is when most customers get their cars washed, you emphasize, showing a *BAR CHART* (Figure 1-3) you have constructed from records of cars washed over an eight-week period.

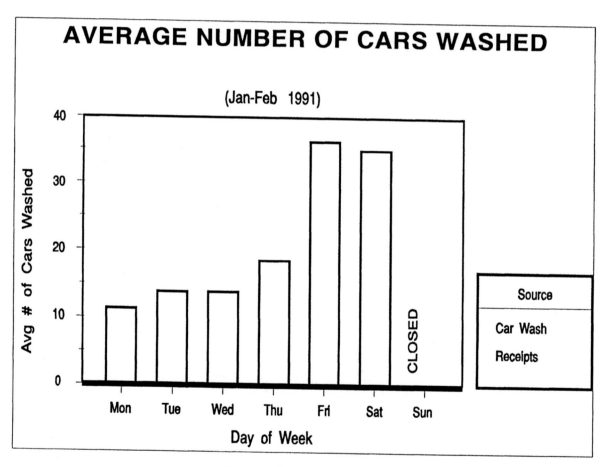

Figure 1-3. Bar Chart

You also tell the owner that you need more towels and another clothes dryer to dry the towels after use. To prove this point, you describe how you arrived at this conclusion. You begin by telling the owner how you keep track of the average time it takes to wash a car using a *LINE GRAPH* (Figure 1-4). You noticed that the average wash time increased every time it got busy. In other words, when there were more cars to be washed, it took longer to wash them. To determine why this was happening, you decided to look in more detail at major steps involved in the car wash process.

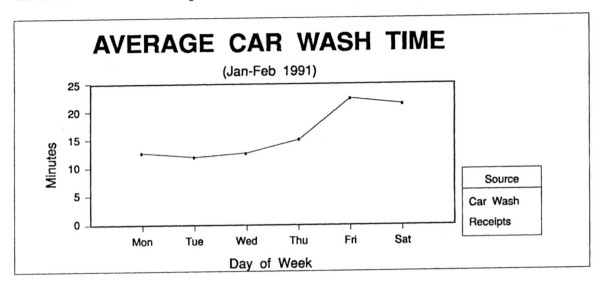

Figure 1-4. Line Graph

There are five major steps involved with washing a car. You collected data on each of them using a *CHECKSHEET* (Figure 1-5). Looking at this data, you

TIME TO COMPLETE CAR WASH
(Minutes)

Step Day,Time	1 Vacuum	2 Tires	3 Wash	4 Blow Dry	5 Hand Dry	TOTAL
Mon, 10 am	3	1	3	1	4	12
Tue, 9 am	2	1	3	1	4	11
Wed, 10 am	3	2	3	1	3	12
Thu, 10 am	4	1	3	1	6	15
Fri, 10 am	3	1	3	1	14	22
Sat, 11 am	4	1	3	1	10	19
Mon, 2 pm	3	2	3	1	3	12
Tue, 2 pm	3	1	3	1	3	11
Wed, 3 pm	4	1	3	1	4	13
Thu, 4 pm	2	1	3	1	8	15
Fri, 3 pm	3	2	3	1	11	20
Sat, 4 pm	3	1	3	1	13	21
TOTAL	37	15	36	12	83	183

Figure 1-5. Checksheet

determined that hand drying the car takes the most time. After *INTERVIEWING* several of your employees, you determined that at busy times there weren't enough dry towels available, consequently more drying time was required. You remind the owner that reducing the time it takes to wash a car is important to the customer by referring to "quick service" in Figure 1-2.

Summarizing your findings to the owner, you state that the cost of the advertising will be $10,000, and the dryer and towels will cost $1,000. How do you think the owner will react?

Maybe you are thinking, "Sounds great, and even makes sense, but it wouldn't work here. Where I work the boss wouldn't listen." Well, don't be so sure. More and more these days, management is challenged to be innovative. They need employees who feel encouraged to contribute their experience and knowledge. After all, things are changing. How long ago was it that you couldn't expect mail to be delivered from New York to San Francisco overnight? How long ago was it that you couldn't send a written message to someone over a phone line? How long ago was it that products made in Japan were considered junk?

Being Part Of The Change

Things do change, and it is people who make them change: people who are willing to make a difference make things change; people who desire to become part of the solution, not part of the problem. The following words sum this up well:

There are three kinds of people:

1. People who make things happen.

2. People who have things happen to them.

3. People who wonder what happened.

What kind of person are you? The tools for quality improvement provide you with an opportunity to make a difference. The tools are so basic that you might discount their inherent potential, until you try them for yourself and find out how powerful they can be when applied correctly—just like in the example with the car wash.

Applying the tools, you will begin to feel that your job has meaning. You will feel good about yourself. In fact, a number of positive outcomes will result from using the tools successfully. Some of them are shown in Figure 1-6.

WHAT YOU CAN EXPECT FROM USING THE TOOLS

Using the tools for quality improvement, you will be able to:

- Define problems in a clear and concise manner
- Establish priorities for problems
- Analyze problems to identify causes
- Gather useful data
- Involve others critical to improvement
- Identify and implement solutions needed to correct problems

---

Figure 1-6

Familiarity And Understanding

One good thing about the education you received in school—you probably are already familiar with the basic math skills required to use the tools for quality improvement. To find out what I mean by basic, let's look at another example.

Take something simple like going to the grocery store. You start by identifying all of the things that you need. This is similar to doing *addition—the total or sum of all the things you need is what you are going to buy. At this point you might discover that something on the list shouldn't be there. You cross it off—subtraction—the sum of what you are going to buy is now different.*

Before you leave for the store you ask yourself the critical question, "Can I afford to buy all of this?" Of course, this means you have to calculate the approximate cost of what you want to buy. "Let's see," you say, "I need 5 cans of soup. At 89 cents a can, that's about $4.50." Now you've used *multiplication.*

Finally, once you've calculated the approximate cost of your grocery bill, you have to determine whether you can *divide* up your paycheck to cover this visit to the store.

Although this example is a little contrived, it makes a point. The tools for quality improvement are just as easy to apply and understand. But to achieve the same level of proficiency with the tools for quality improvement as you have with adding, subtracting, multiplying, and dividing, you must gain experience by using them.

Trial And Error

From my experience, people learn best by doing. You can read this book over and over until you have memorized every word on every page, but you won't have progressed much toward becoming a proficient user of the tools until you try them several times.

Think about why this is. When you try something new isn't it normal to make mistakes during your initial attempts? This doesn't mean that you can't do it, or that what you are attempting is too difficult. It only means that you need more practice. What about the first time you tried to drive a car, dance, or play tennis? Did you feel uncomfortable? Were you as good the first time as you were later?

As you begin using the tools for quality improvement you will find that they are really not hard to apply. In fact, you can expect to quickly get to the point where using the tools will become second nature. Remember though, like driving, when using the tools it is important to pay attention.

Watch The Details

Consider the grocery store example. What would happen if you didn't correctly add up the list of items you were going to purchase? Can you imagine going to the store's cashier and not having enough money? It's happened to me more than once. As a result I'm more careful.

Being careful with the tools for quality improvement is just as important, because every tool requires an active mind to get the job done. Just using a tool doesn't guarantee accurate results. A tool could be used incorrectly, or not used enough. What's required is for you to maintain an *inquiring mind*. By this I mean you must continue to seek the truth, looking for answers until you are satisfied that you have found something you can believe.

You have seen that to solve a given problem, several of the tools might be used. But using a variety of tools in succession increases the potential for mistakes. Any mistake you make can lead to an incorrect conclusion, even when several correct applications of the tools follow the one instance where a mistake was made. It's like building a house on sand, or using rotted lumber in the framework. Errors made along the way come back to haunt you later.

What would have happened to the car wash manager if he or she had stopped analyzing the car wash process after calculating the average time required to wash a car? The analysis up to this point was fine, but more analysis was necessary to uncover the real cause for the increased time required to dry the cars. If the manager didn't continue to seek the truth, any solutions put in place to improve things would only be addressing a symptom—*the car wash process takes too long*—instead of the cause of the problem—*the time required for hand drying is too long.*

Every time you use a tool, no matter how simple it may seem to apply, be careful to follow the instructions provided in Chapter 3. When you are through using the tool, check your work. There are several ways to do this, depending upon the tool you are using. But the most simple and logical approach is to ask yourself, "Does this make sense?" You will be surprised how often this simple check uncovers errors in application.

Applications

How are the tools for quality improvement to be used? Figure 1-7 offers three major uses for the tools: *analysis, teamwork,* and *data gathering.* Note that some of the tools have more than one major use. For example, *BARRIERS & AIDS* is a tool useful for both analysis and data gathering. Most important though, remember that the tools for quality improvement have no inherent capability. Your understanding and innovative thinking is what makes them useful.

Adding To Your Knowledge Base

When you first learned the multiplication tables, did you ever wonder, "What am I learning this for?" At the time it was just an exercise where you multiplied a column of numbers by the same number to obtain a larger number.

A typical multiplication exercise:

$$3 \times 1 = 3$$

$$3 \times 2 = 6$$

$$3 \times 3 = 9$$

$$3 \times 4 = 12, \text{etc.}$$

Exercises like this required that you remember the larger number and the two numbers that were multiplied together to achieve it. Looking back at the grocery store example, it's easy to see how remembering this information is still valuable. In fact, it has become second nature to you; part of your normal operating behavior; your knowledge base. In the following example, consider how you use the math skills in your knowledge base.

MAJOR USES FOR THE TOOLS

TOOL	USE	TOOL	USE
Bar Chart	Analysis	Interview	Data Gathering
Barriers & Aids	Analysis/Data Gathering	Line Graph	Analysis
Brainstorming	Teamwork/Data Gathering	List Reduction	Teamwork
Cause-and-Effect (Fishbone) Diagram	Analysis	Matrix	Analysis/Data Gathering
Checksheet	Data Gathering/Analysis	Pareto Chart	Analysis
Flowchart	Analysis	Pie Chart	Analysis
Histogram	Analysis	Survey	Data Gathering

Figure 1-7

You have a $5 bill. You enter the local convenience store and walk up to the beverage cooler. You want to buy as many bottles of cola as you can with the money you have. Do you ask yourself, "Should I use addition, subtraction, multiplication, or division to determine the answer?" Probably not. Why? Because making simple calculations like this comes so naturally that you really don't think about the type of math you are using.

Achieving the same level of familiarity with the tools for quality improvement should be your personal goal. These tools are just as basic, and you will find they are just as valuable. Once you get to the point where the tools are part of your knowledge base, both your value as an employee and your contribution to the work will be dramatically increased.

A Changed Approach

When you get to the point where using the tools for quality improvement is second nature, your approach to work will have changed. You will say "I can" more often than "I can't." You will approach problems differently, too. You will ask "why" more often. You will look for the reasons problems occur. Poor quality and service will bother you. You will be less frustrated with your own work, though, because you will know how to make improvements.

A little story emphasizes this point. I had just bought a new car—a Japanese model. I was visiting my father when he asked, "Why didn't you buy an American car?"

I wasn't prepared for this question, but I thought about it and told him. "Dad, do you remember the last car I bought?"

"Of course," he said. The car was an American model; the first new car I ever owned. He was happy I had reached the level of financial stability to afford it.

"Well, as soon as I bought it I started a list of the things that needed repair," I told him.

"That's a good idea son," he said approvingly.

Then I made my point. "Since I sold that car and bought this one six months ago, I haven't had to start a list. In fact, I don't even know the service manager's name, because I haven't been there."

The reality struck him. He started to look at the Japanese car differently. He even looked under the hood, wondering how it was put together; maybe there was a clue as to why it didn't have defects.

I've since done a reasonable amount of study concerning the success of Japanese companies in the marketplace. One of my findings is that in Japan, employees work very hard at thinking differently about their work.

A defective part in most American cars will be replaced with a new one. It's even a law in most states that the defective part be given to you for review so that you can see that it is defective and should be replaced. In Japan this type of law could not be enforced, because manufacturers would not want to give you the defective part. Instead, they would want to keep it, to study it in order to determine why it failed. Then they would want to correct the cause of the defect so that it would never occur again. This is the reason products from Japan are so renowned for their quality.

Feeling Empowered

In Japan, analyzing problems and correcting them is part of the job. To accomplish this work, each employee is taught the basic tools provided in this book. Armed with these tools for quality improvement, employees go about their work with an attitude of pride and empowerment. They feel responsible for the products they produce and the services they provide for their customers.

Japan has no patent on these tools. You and I can use them freely. They can open up doors that may have been closed to you for a long time. It sounds unbelievable doesn't it? But it's that simple. The trick is to begin thinking differently. Believe that you can make a difference and use the tools to help state your case.

Why go home dissatisfied and unhappy because things aren't the way they should be at work? Why ignore problems on the job when you can empower yourself to make the changes that are necessary?

The handle to the door leading to more satisfying and rewarding work is in your hands right now.

Two

A Systematic Approach

In the previous chapter you read that the tools for quality improvement can benefit you in a variety of ways. In this chapter you will learn how to apply the tools in order to derive the most benefit from them. You will find that the tools can be used by one person working alone, or by a group of people, sometimes referred to as a work team. Finally, you will learn that the tools can be applied in association with five problem-solving steps to improve or eliminate problems related to quality.

Actually, the number of potential uses for the tools is limited only by your ability to think of new and different applications. The tools can be used to solve problems, provide clarity, develop understanding, and help with decision making. Like the instruments a doctor uses in the operating room, or the screwdrivers, wrenches, and pliers in a mechanic's tool kit, each of the tools for quality improvement is ready to do its part to accomplish an objective. All that's needed is your skill in applying the tools correctly.

Use Of The Tools By Teams

Remember the old saying, "Two heads are better than one"? Well, consider the power of five to seven heads working with a common set of tools to accomplish an objective. Work teams use the tools for quality improvement to capture their collective intelligence and experience. They use the tools to come to agreement on issues, analyze complex situations, and plan, and then implement actions. In fact, when a small group or work team gets together to solve a quality problem, the effectiveness of the tools is enhanced.

Some of the tools for quality improvement are more effective when applied by a work team rather than an individual. *BRAINSTORMING*, for example, is a tool that can be used by one person, but when a team uses brainstorming, the results are dramatically increased. In fact, many of the tools are designed to capture the collective thoughts of several people. The tools for quality improvement help work teams utilize their combined experience and intelligence to go beyond what would be accomplished by one person working alone.

Work teams are effective when people who know the most about a problem are involved. But first, workers must be educated in the use of the tools so that they can apply them correctly. A work team's successful application of the tools helps motivate them by removing the frustration that occurs when hard work alone fails to improve quality and achieve production expectations. Management benefits from work teams, too, when workers recommend alternatives and solutions to product and service quality problems.

Applying The Tools To Solve Quality Problems

Solving problems related to quality is probably the most common application of the tools for quality improvement. Quality problems occur when a product or service is not meeting the needs and agreed-upon expectations of its intended customer(s). Maybe the service is being provided later than the customer desires, or the reliability of the service is not dependable. It could be that the product has defects that render it unusable for the customer. Whatever the type of quality problem, the tools for quality improvement can be applied to reduce or eliminate them.

Quality problems are usually identified when data are collected and displayed using one of the tools. In Figure 2-1 a *LINE GRAPH* is used to display an increasing trend in the number of defects per thousand of part X.

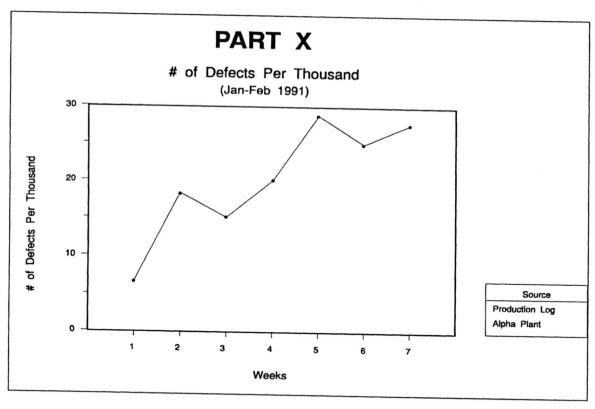

Figure 2-1. Line Graph

The reasons for the increase in defects may be many and varied. Workers often feel frustrated when they are shown data like this because they have been doing their best, but the data prove that their best is not good enough. The only way to reduce their frustration is to turn the situation around—to reduce the number of defective parts being produced. But what can be done?

Too often, management, feeling pressured to change a negative situation, will get on the "quality bandwagon." They might post signs with quality slogans, and even show their workers graphs like the one in the figure. But after a period of time, as both workers and management watch the numbers being posted for the next period, little progress has been made. Why? Not from lack of effort, and not because management didn't identify that a problem exists. The reason the situation didn't improve is because real action was not taken to change things.

Let's look at another situation to see why just identifying the problem is not enough. Assume that your car was not starting properly. For the past several weeks, each morning as you prepared to go to work, you got into the car anxiously wondering whether or not the car was going to start. Recognizing that there is a problem, you tell the car that you expect it to start. In fact, you tell your family, the people at work, and anyone else who will listen that the car has a problem. This done, will the car start when you want it to? How can it? Because you told it to? Is telling a car to improve and informing others of this any different from telling a machine, process, or employee to improve when the capability to make corrections is missing?

When there are problems with quality, steps must be taken to identify and correct the *causes* of the problem. The problem with your car will not go away without the skilled hand of a mechanic using his or her tools properly. The same is true for problems with quality. Tools must be used by skilled employees, trained to apply them properly to make the needed improvements.

Using The Tools With A Systematic Approach

The tools' potential to reduce or eliminate quality problems is increased when problems are addressed systematically, using a consistent and analytic approach. *Consistency* in approach implies that the methodology shouldn't change just because the problem changes. In fact, the steps followed should be the same every time a problem is addressed. This helps build the confidence of those who are applying the steps, and reinforces a new way of thinking about problems. The approach should also be *analytic*, using steps that lead to a careful review of a problem and tools that develop a worthwhile solution.

Using a consistent, analytic process to solve problems is not a revolutionary idea. I first came in contact with it in school when a teacher asked my class to read an article by Henry Margenau and David Bergamini. The article was published in the December 1964 issue of *Fortune Magazine*. Entitled "The Scientific Method," the article sounded technical, but turned out to be a logical approach to bringing order out of confusion. Messrs. Margenau and Bergamini described the scientific method as a combination of the process of reflective thinking and the methods of science. Since my school days, I have seen many variations on the approach they described; most are similar in scope to the five problem-solving steps shown in Figure 2.2.

FIVE PROBLEM-SOLVING STEPS		
Step	**Actions**	**Useful Tools**
1. IDENTIFY THE PROBLEM	a. Identify something that needs improvement b. Show the need for improvement in measurable terms c. State the problem d. Establish an interim target and a date for achieving this improvement	Brainstorming, Interview, Survey, List Reduction, Matrix
2. ANALYZE	a. Identify root cause(s) of the problem b. Verify each root cause c. Identify the root cause(s) most responsible for the problem	Cause-and-Effect Diagram, Flowchart, Pareto Chart, Brainstorming, Checksheet
3. EVALUATE ALTERNATIVES	a. Identify actions that will reduce or eliminate the root cause(s) b. Determine which actions will lead to the targeted level of improvement c. Plan the implementation of selected solutions	Brainstorming, Interview, Survey
4. TEST-IMPLEMENT	a. Implement the plan b. Help the solutions succeed c. Show measurable improvement d. If improvement is not evident, return to step 1c	Line Graph, Pareto Chart, Pie Chart, Bar Chart, Histogram, Checksheet
5. STANDARDIZE	a. Ensure that your solutions are made permanent b. Determine if the solutions will be effective elsewhere	Flowchart, Brainstorming

Figure 2-2

The steps provide a structural framework to use in conjunction with the tools. This enables users to have a meaningful impact on their work. The five problem-solving steps appear sensible and logical, but take a minute to evaluate them further. Do these steps offer a practical, sensible way to arrive at a worthwhile solution? Consider a quality problem you are having at work or home, then walk through each of the steps in your mind.

1. **Identify the Problem:** Clearly state what needs improvement.

2. **Analyze:** Determine what causes the problem to occur.

3. **Evaluate Alternatives:** Identify and select actions to reduce or eliminate the problem.

4. **Test Implement:** Implement these actions on a trial basis to determine their effectiveness.

5. **Standardize:** Ensure that useful actions are preserved.

If you believe that these five steps can lead to improved quality, then you have taken the first step necessary to make this problem-solving process effective. Next you must begin to develop your understanding of the five steps and the actions associated with them. As you perform each step, the tools for quality improvement are the instruments you will use to organize and collect information, analyze it, and display your findings.

Linkage Between Steps

As you consider the problem-solving steps, notice how each step leads to the next with a specific output. For example, one of the outputs of Step 1—*Identify The Problem*—is a problem statement. In Step 2—*Analyze*—this problem statement becomes the basis for identifying the cause(s) of the problem. Therefore, the first step, once completed, results in an output that will be used in the second step. This same pattern holds true for all the steps.

The output(s) for each step are developed by completing the *actions* associated with them. Step 1—*Identify The Problem*—requires that four actions be completed. Each action explains what must be done to execute the step. By completing all of the actions carefully, elements of reflective thinking and the scientific approach are built into your activities, ensuring that the result is reasonable and sensible.

Understanding The Problem-Solving Steps

The actions associated with each step in the problem-solving process are not difficult to complete, but some explanation can be helpful. Throughout the rest of this chapter, each of the steps will be covered in detail, with guidelines provided to help you effectively complete the actions associated with each step.

STEP 1: Identify The Problem

ACTION 1A:

Identify something that needs improvement.

In most work environments, problems, or improvement opportunities as they are sometimes called, are easily identified. But choosing just *any* problem may not reap the benefits your efforts deserve. To get the most out of the time that will be invested completing the problem-solving steps, focus on a *customer-related* problem. Customer-related problems pose the biggest threat for any business. When customers are dissatisfied with a product or service, they will go elsewhere. And when enough customers make that choice, a business fails, putting everyone's job in jeopardy.

How do you identify customer-related problems? A tool for quality improvement that is most useful for generating ideas is *BRAINSTORMING*. It is best used by a team of employees to identify customer-related problems like:

- recurring errors in a work process
- visible failures
- inconsistent performance

Other tools for quality improvement that can help are the *SURVEY* and *INTERVIEW*. By using these tools customer-related problems surface quickly as you listen to:

- comments and feedback from your customers
- recommendations from others—fellow workers, the boss, other departments, suppliers, etc.

It is possible that a large list of customer-related problems will be identified using these tools. To reduce this list so that there are only a few problems to choose from, *LIST REDUCTION,* another Tool for Quality Improvement, is used.

After reducing a list using List Reduction, it is still necessary to select one problem from those remaining. This selection is accomplished using a *MATRIX*. The matrix is a valuable tool for comparing the remaining problems against a set of criteria such as those listed in Figure 2-3.

PROBLEM-SELECTION MATRIX

Problems \ Criteria	Within Our Control/ Influence	Potential For Cost Savings	Number of Customers Affected	Signifi- cance of Problem	TOTAL
1 Too many defects	3	3	3	3	12
2 Absenteeism is high	1	2	2	3	8
3 Equipment breakdowns	1	3	3	2	9
4 Water cooler too far away	3	1	1	1	6

3 = High   2 = Medium   1 = Low

Figure 2-3. Matrix

ACTION 1B:

Show the need for improvement in measurable terms.

Once a customer-related problem has been identified, it must be defined in measurable terms for clarification. This is accomplished by:

- *gathering* information about the problem area, and
- *organizing* this data so that the nature of the problem is clear.

Gathering information is accomplished using the *CHECKSHEET*, another tool for quality improvement; see Figure 2-4.

TIME TO COMPLETE CAR WASH
(Minutes)

Day,Time \ Step	[1] Vacuum	[2] Tires	[3] Wash	[4] Blow Dry	[5] Hand Dry	TOTAL
Mon, 10 am	3	1	3	1	4	12
Tue, 9 am	2	1	3	1	4	11
Wed, 10 am	3	2	3	1	3	12
Thu, 10 am	4	1	3	1	6	15
Fri, 10 am	3	1	3	1	14	22
Sat, 11 am	4	1	3	1	10	19
Mon, 2 pm	3	2	3	1	3	12
Tue, 2 pm	3	1	3	1	3	11
Wed, 3 pm	4	1	3	1	4	13
Thu, 4 pm	2	1	3	1	8	15
Fri, 3 pm	3	2	3	1	11	20
Sat, 4 pm	3	1	3	1	13	21
TOTAL	37	15	36	12	83	183

Figure 2-4. Checksheet

Organizing the data gathered with a checksheet is done to clarify the problem, and to show improvement by comparing current performance with future performance. This involves identifying an indicator to communicate the need for improvement. The indicator may be one already in use, or one developed for this purpose.

The following tools are commonly used as indicators: *LINE GRAPHS, PARETO CHARTS, HISTOGRAMS, BAR and PIE CHARTS.*

In Figure 2-5 a bar chart is used to indicate the most active day of the week at a car wash.

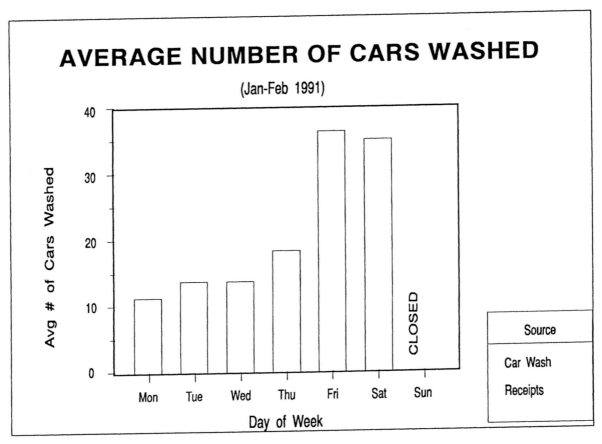

Figure 2-5. Bar Chart

ACTION 1C:

State the problem.

Having defined the problem in measurable terms, it can then be stated in a manner that clarifies the situation. Most problem statements are stated in sweeping, inexact terms when first identified. For example: *The water temperature is too hot.*

But a problem defined in measurable terms can be restated so that the nature of the problem is clarified: *56% of the water temperature readings over the past four weeks were more than 10 degrees above the acceptable level.* This problem statement is specific and will serve to focus the efforts of those who set out to solve the problem.

The guidelines in Figure 2-6 will assist with the development of problem statements that clarify the nature of the problem.

GUIDELINES FOR DEVELOPING A PROBLEM STATEMENT

The problem statement should

1. Be specific

The statement, *Administrative errors are excessive*, is a problem statement that is too broad and unclear. This problem would be better stated: *Billing errors are 15 percent higher than this same period last year*. By the same token the problem statement, *Billing errors occurring on Tuesday morning have increased by 5 percent*, is too specific. It does not take into consideration errors that might be occurring on other days of the week.

2. Describe a problem, not a symptom

The statement, *Department morale is low*, is a symptom, not a problem. It suggests that other problems exist. What is the problem that results in low morale? Is it too many hours worked? Or is this a symptom of a staffing problem? The analysis completed in problem-solving Step 2 will verify whether you are dealing with a problem or a symptom.

3. Relate the current situation to what is desired

The problem statement, *Order processing costs are 20 percent higher than our competitors*, is better than, *Order processing is too costly*, because it includes an indication of the desired level of improvement.

4. Be free of causes and solutions

The problem statement, *Service response time is the cause of customer dissatisfaction*, identifies a potential cause of the problem. But service response time may only be a part of the overall customer dissatisfaction problem. Equipment performance could be the root cause of the problem, and be overlooked because the problem statement focuses on response time.

Figure 2-6

ACTION 1D:

Establish an interim target and a date for achieving this improvement.

A target defines a desired performance level. Setting a target includes the assumption that time will elapse before the desired level of performance is achieved. For this reason a target and date for achieving it must be established simultaneously.

You will find that setting a realistic target is difficult this early in the application of the problem-solving steps. At this point very little is known about the cause(s) of the problem, making it hard to project a target level of improvement. Still, an interim target should be established as motivation, and for planning purposes, by the individual or team working on the problem. The guidelines in Figure 2-7 will help, but keep in mind that the interim target can be changed once the analysis is completed in Step 2. The new target will reflect your increased understanding of the problem being addressed.

GUIDELINES FOR SETTING TARGETS

1. **Targets should be expressed quantitatively.**

   The use of percentages is a common method for describing the desired improvement. A good example is, *Reduce order processing time by 20 percent*.

2. **Targets should be aggressive.**

   Most problems can be classified as either *zero* or *reduction*. *Zero problems* reflect a need to eliminate a situation. *Customer complaints have increased by 23% over the past six months*, is a good example of a zero problem. Customer complaints can be eliminated. An aggressive interim improvement target for a zero problem is 50 percent.

   Reduction problems involve areas where improvement is possible, but elimination of the problem is unlikely. Problems associated with time and cost are typical reduction problems. An aggressive interim target for a reduction problem is 20 to 30 percent lower than current levels.

3. **Targets should be changed as the situation changes.**

   Things change, and the resulting circumstances require flexibility. For example, if an established target cannot be achieved because anticipated resources were used elsewhere, the target will probably have to be adjusted.

4. **Establish a long-term target and define intermediate targets.**

   Intermediate targets provide for annual monitoring and goal setting. For example, if an ultimate target were to achieve a 25% reduction in invoice processing time by 1995, intermediate targets should be set for each of the years leading up to this target date.

Figure 2-7

STEP 2: Analyze

ACTION 2A:

Identify root cause(s) of the problem.

In Step 1 of the problem-solving process, a problem statement was developed that clarifies the nature of the problem. In Step 2, the causes of this problem are identified. These causes are commonly referred to as *root causes*. A root cause is the underlying reason that a problem occurs. If a root cause is removed or eliminated, the problem, or at least a portion of it, would also be removed.

Identifying root causes is sometimes difficult because *symptoms* of the problem often look like root causes. A symptom is evidence that a problem exists, but removing it won't result in the problem being removed. See Figure 2-6, item 2, for more on the difference between a symptom and a problem.

When a problem is recognized, many ideas surface as to the cause of the problem. These assumptions are sometimes accurate, sometimes not. It is valuable to investigate each idea, but not to limit the analysis by not allowing that other causes may exist. Identifying root causes requires a determined investigation that goes beyond previous assumptions.

For example, a work team agrees that *Slow service response time* is causing the problem: "74% of the customers are dissatisfied with our repair service." If the team came to this conclusion without doing additional analysis, they could overlook other potential causes of the problem. Response time may only be a part of the overall customer dissatisfaction problem. Poor equipment performance due to a problem occurring when the equipment was manufactured could be the root cause of the problem. Without a determined investigation, the problem would go uncorrected because the analysis only focused on service response time.

Identifying the root cause(s) requires gathering and analyzing data relating to the problem. Data provide a guide for action. From data you learn facts. With the facts, you can make the best decision. Some guidelines for collecting data are listed in Figure 2-8.

GUIDELINES FOR COLLECTING DATA

1. Establish a purpose before collecting data.

Stating a purpose directs you to collect only the data you will need.
It will also help you arrange the data to be more useful. Begin by asking
the question, "What do we want the data for?" Then, collect the data that
serve your purpose. Data are usually collected to:

- monitor the activities in a work process
- analyze for nonconformance
- monitor process output
- make comparisons

2. Determine if the indicators are reliable.

Find out where the data came from. Check to see if the data are accurate.
If they aren't, their analytical value is questionable. Ensuring the reliability
of data includes:

- checking the instruments and materials used to take the
  measurements
- determining if the methods used to take the measurements are
  consistently followed

3. Track all the data needed.

Collect enough data to perform a thorough analysis.

4. Record the data carefully.

Sloppy work means rework later. Develop a checksheet to collect the
data, and:

- prepare the checksheet so that the information you want is easily
  obtained
- post the data neatly
- identify the origin of the data

  -time, date, etc.?
  -who was doing the work, what machine, etc.?
  -who took the measurement?

Figure 2-8

As you analyze the data collected, keep in mind that there may be one or more root causes. Make a thorough analysis of the data, and collect additional data if necessary to identify all of the root causes. Tools for quality improvement useful for identifying root causes are *CAUSE-AND-EFFECT DIAGRAM, FLOWCHART, BRAINSTORMING, CHECKSHEET,* and *PARETO CHART.*

Using these tools you may discover additional information that requires going back to Step 1 to change the problem statement. Taking this small step back before moving ahead is normal. It ensures the continuity and logic of your problem-solving efforts, and reflects your deeper understanding of the problem being addressed.

ACTION 2B:

Verify each root cause.

This action is taken to confirm any assumptions about the root cause(s) of the problem you have identified. It involves the following:

1. Isolate the cause to be verified.

2. Reduce or eliminate this cause.

3. Determine the effect of your action on the problem.

If the problem is measurably reduced or eliminated, then a root cause has been identified. If the desired effect does not occur, and no measurable improvement is evident, then a root cause has not been identified and further analysis is required. A *MATRIX* is a tool that can be used to summarize your efforts to verify each of the identified root causes. Figure 2-9 shows how the potential root causes identified in a *CAUSE-AND-EFFECT DIAGRAM* have been verified and communicated using a matrix.

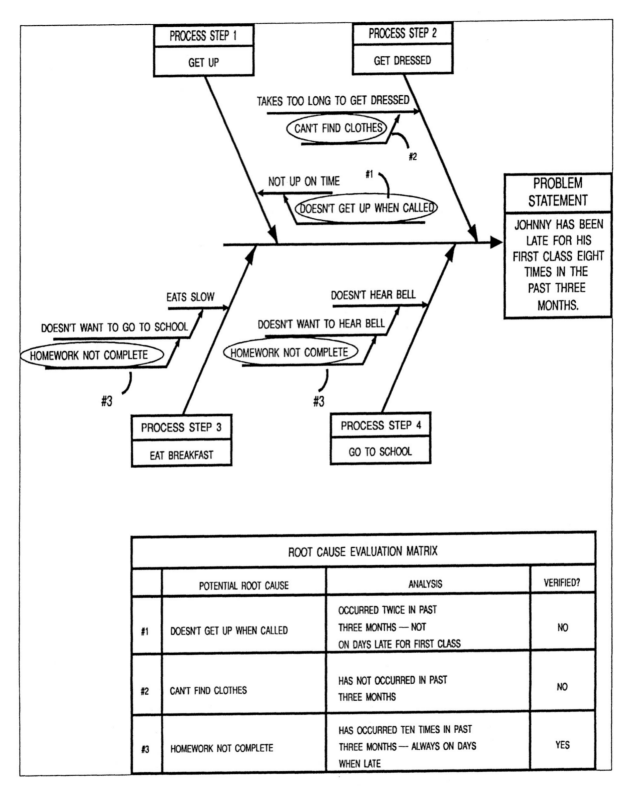

Figure 2-9. Cause-and-Effect Diagram

ACTION 2C:

Identify the root cause(s) most responsible for the problem.

When more than one root cause is identified, further analysis is required to establish the root cause(s) most responsible for the problem. This additional analysis is valuable because it helps to focus and optimize the resources available to reduce or eliminate the problem. For example, if reducing or eliminating one of three verified root causes will achieve a 95% improvement, then that root cause should be addressed first, because expending resources to improve the other two root causes cannot achieve comparable results. Tools for quality improvement that can be used to complete this action are the *CHECKSHEET, HISTOGRAM, BAR CHART* and *PARETO CHART.*

Figure 2-10 is an example in which a Pareto chart has been used to clarify why one root cause was selected over two others. This chart was constructed to address the problem: *Overtime has increased by 25% during the past four weeks.*

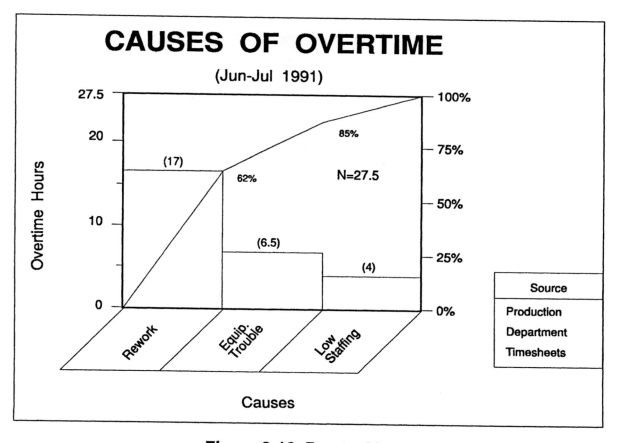

Figure 2-10. Pareto Chart

STEP 3: Evaluate Alternatives

ACTION 3A:

Identify actions that will reduce or eliminate the root cause(s).

When this step in the problem-solving process has been reached, the nature of the problem and what is causing it to occur have both been established. It's time to consider actions that will reduce (reduction problem) or eliminate (zero problem) these root causes. (See Figure 2-7 for an explanation of these two types of problems.)

Several alternatives may already have been identified before reaching this step. The tendency is to consider only these alternatives, but this common mistake excludes other solutions that may be more effective and less costly to implement. Figure 2-11 provides some key points to remember when developing a *comprehensive* list of alternative solutions. Tools for quality improvement that will help produce a comprehensive list of ideas are *BRAINSTORMING, INTERVIEW,* and *SURVEY.*

GUIDELINES FOR DEVELOPING ALTERNATIVE SOLUTIONS

1. **Be creative—identify as many potential actions as possible.**

   Having many alternative solutions is valuable. It's hard to predict which solutions will work and which won't. You should identify as many ways to solve the problem as possible in order to select those that will work best.

2. **Don't be constrained by current practice.**

   "That's the way we've always done it" are seven words that should never be said together. Learn to think outside of the way things are. Think about what could be. Get ideas from others, not as close to the problem, who may have ideas you might not have considered.

3. **Be supportive.**

   A major barrier in the development of new ideas is the reaction of others to our thoughts. When people react negatively and put down our ideas, we tend to retreat. When our ideas are accepted, we are more willing to share our thoughts.

Figure 2-11

ACTION 3B:

Determine which actions will lead to the targeted level of improvement.

When a comprehensive list of alternative solutions has been developed, select those that will reduce or eliminate the verified root cause(s) of the problem. To accomplish this, the list of alternatives is evaluated for potential effectiveness using a *MATRIX*. Each alternative is compared against a set of criteria, such as those listed in Figure 2-12.

FACTORS TO CONSIDER WHEN CHOOSING SOLUTIONS

Criteria	What to Evaluate
Effectiveness	Has this been tried before? Will it solve all or part of the problem? Will it achieve the target for improvement?
Feasibility	Can we implement this solution? Is it practical?
Timeliness	How fast will it work? Is it a long- or short-term solution? Can we afford to wait?
Customer-oriented	Does it satisfy identified customer requirements? Will it improve service quality?
Efficiency	Is this solution cost effective?

Figure 2-12

Keep in mind that more than one solution may be required to achieve the interim target established in Step 1d. For example, assume that you want to reduce heat loss in an office building by 20 percent (the interim target). If your proposed solution, caulking the windows, accounts for 5 percent of the heat loss, you must determine if other solutions are available, because the caulking solution alone won't achieve the interim target.

Change the interim target if necessary. Review the interim target established in Step 1d. Having selected one or more solutions to reduce or eliminate the problem, you should now confirm whether or not this target is still valid. Change the target based on the potential of the solutions you have selected to reduce or eliminate the problem. Determine the amount of improvement that would be achieved if your solutions were implemented, and change the target, if necessary, to reflect your increased understanding of the problem being addressed. Your actions may result in a higher or lower target level.

ACTION 3C:

Plan the implementation of selected solutions.

Begin this activity by evaluating the impact of your proposed actions. Consider the major elements of most processes: People, Materials, Methods, and Machines. Some ideas are listed in Figure 2-13.

Major Elements	What to Consider
People	Whose support will be needed to successfully implement your solutions?
Materials	Will your solutions require that new or different materials be utilized? Where do they come from? Who will procure them?
Methods	How will those involved learn how to implement what you propose? The solutions you plan to implement represent a *change* from the way things are currently being performed. How will you know if your solutions are working? The effectiveness of each solution must be measured to identify those solutions that are effective and those that aren't.
Machinery/ Equipment	Will your solutions require that new or different equipment be utilized? Where will it come from? Who will procure it? How will others be trained to operate it?

Figure 2-13. Major Elements Of Most Processes

Before developing a formal plan, take time to consider any factors that might represent an obstacle to the successful implementation of your solutions. Then, develop and include in your plan a set of countering actions to overcome these barriers. A tool for quality improvement that is useful for this type of evaluation is *BARRIERS & AIDS*. Using this tool you can identify *barriers* that might hinder the implementation of your solutions, and *aids* that will support what you propose to do. For every barrier identified, actions must be planned that will counter, or offset, this potential negative influence. An example of *Barriers & Aids* is provided in Figure 2-14.

From the information generated in the Barriers & Aids analysis, you can now develop a thorough implementation plan.

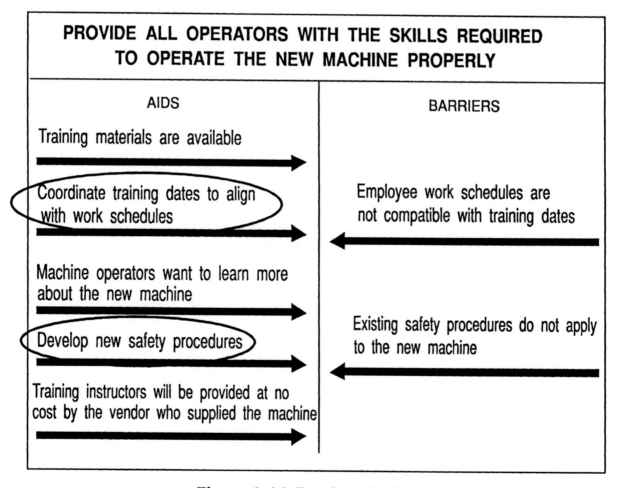

Figure 2-14. Barriers & Aids

Carefully planning the implementation of your identified solutions increases the potential for these solutions to achieve the desired result. Careful planning includes the elements listed in Figure 2-15.

ELEMENTS OF PLANNING

The objective is clearly stated: The overall reason for developing the plan is understood by everyone involved.

Each activity is defined: The specific actions required to fully implement each solution are identified.

Responsibility is assigned: A person is identified to perform each activity, and assignments are made clear.

Due dates are established: Each activity is given a target date for completion with the date made part of the assigned responsibility.

Figure 2-15

The *MATRIX* is a useful tool for organizing a thorough implementation plan. Figure 2-16 is an example of a plan that clearly communicates what is proposed and who is responsible. A plan documented in this manner can be easily monitored for progress and used later as a record of the actions undertaken.

IMPLEMENTATION PLAN

What	How	Who	When	Notes
Research/recommend work gloves and glove clips	Check with vendors Ensure that products are quality and price competitive Coordinate with purchasing supervisor	Tom Tom Tom	3/3/91 3/3/91 3/3/91	Complete Complete Complete
Develop procedure for issuing work gloves and clips	Develop procedures Ensure compatibility with existing procedures	Ken Ken	3/17/91 3/17/91	
Add work gloves and clips to storeroom inventory	Ensure space is available Add items to inventory control	Al Becky	3/17/91 3/17/91	
Storeroom to issue work gloves and glove clips	Get Mr. Steadman's approval	Team	3/24/91	
Communicate new procedure to affected employees	Draft safety bulletin from Mr. Steadman Discuss with union representative Include in safety procedures	Becky Al Ken	3/17/91 3/17/91 3/17/91	

Figure 2-16

STEP 4: Test-Implement

ACTION 4A:

Implement the plan.

Reaching this step in the problem-solving process is an exciting time. The carefully and logically developed plan of action is ready to be implemented. It's time to realize the value of your work, to observe a reduction or elimination of the problem you have been studying. The first implementation of your plans should be undertaken on a trial basis. A test implementation will provide you and others an opportunity to assess the effectiveness of your solutions and the plan to implement them. A test implementation also provides useful information that can be used to ensure the success of the actual implementation when it occurs.

Most likely, before a test implementation is possible, someone's approval will have to be obtained. Gaining this approval should be easy because the tools for quality improvement will help to communicate your findings clearly and convince others that your work is thorough and logical.

ACTION 4B:

Help the solutions succeed.

Even when a thorough implementation plan is developed, unanticipated problems can occur. Encountering problems during the test implementation is not unusual. Maybe those responsible for implementing your solutions don't understand, or aren't trained to carry out your plan. Sometimes those responsible for implementing the solutions use the new practice for a little while, then drop it in favor of the old way—because the old way was easier or more familiar. These and other problems must be addressed in order to facilitate the plan's success. The guidelines in Figure 2-17 will help ensure the effectiveness of your solutions.

ENSURING EFFECTIVE SOLUTIONS

Communicate the Plan: Ensure that anyone affected by a solution understands the reason for its being implemented. Getting people involved early increases the potential for change to be accepted.

Monitor Plan Implementation: Make certain the solutions are implemented according to plan. Verify that the materials, training, management support, etc. that were part of the solution are carried out as intended.

Reinforce Each Other: Look for ways to help those involved with implementing the solutions. Recognize that these solutions represent a change, and that change is sometimes difficult for people to handle. Offer encouragement frequently and assistance as required.

Adjust When Necessary: If the implementation plan is achieving the desired results, then the plan is working well. If it isn't, then determine why and make adjustments. It may become necessary to modify the plan. If so, consider who and what will be impacted, then work with those involved to make the necessary changes.

Figure 2-17

ACTION 4C:

Show measurable improvement.

The most convincing way to prove that implemented solutions are working is to show measurable improvement in the problem area. The best method of displaying this measurable improvement is by using the tools for quality improvement, like a *LINE GRAPH, PARETO CHART, PIE CHART, BAR CHART, HISTOGRAM,* or *CHECKSHEET.* Show the effectiveness of implemented solutions with an overall indicator, and show the effectiveness of each individual solution with an indicator for that solution.

The overall indicator is the one that was used in Step 1b to show the need for improvement in measurable terms. It should now be updated by posting current data to reflect the effect of your implemented solutions.

When more than one solution has been implemented, each solution must be monitored independently. This enables you to determine which solutions are working effectively to reduce or eliminate the problem, and to communicate this information to others.

ACTION 4D:

If measurable improvement is not evident, return to Step 1c.

The problem-solving steps and tools for quality improvement will not always reduce or eliminate the problem as planned. This is unfortunate but true, and can occur for several reasons. Three of the most common are (1) a poor problem statement, (2) the analysis was insufficient or inaccurate, and (3) the verification of root causes was inadequate.

If the test implementation of solutions does not achieve the desired level of improvement, then look for errors in your application of the problem-solving steps or tools for quality improvement beginning with Step 1c. Sometimes it's useful to call in a person familiar with the problem-solving steps and tools to help with this review. A fresh perspective may uncover errors you can't see because of your proximity to the problem.

STEP 5: Standardize

ACTION 5A :

Ensure that your solutions are made permanent.

Problems sometimes appear to correct themselves when they are under the spotlight created by the problem-solving steps. This pseudo improvement usually occurs because the work activities related to the problem are being performed more carefully when under investigation. Once the investigation is over, or the spotlight is turned off, work activities return to normal and the problem can reappear.

To verify that the "spotlight effect" is not the only reason your solutions are succeeding, continue to monitor your implemented solutions. Note any changes to the indicators you have established for each solution. After verifying that your solutions are having the desired effect, some of the monitoring may be discontinued. But you will want to make certain that the solutions are incorporated into the work process so that the problem doesn't reoccur. Following the steps outlined in Figure 2-18 will maintain the gains achieved by your solutions.

STEPS FOR MAINTAINING THE GAINS

1. **Make Periodic Checks:** The overall indicator established in Step 1b should be monitored routinely.

2. **Clarify Work Activities:** Develop a picture of how the work is to be performed. A tool for quality improvement useful for this purpose is the *FLOWCHART.* A flowchart documents the steps involved with the work and clarifies how the work is to be performed.

3. **Develop and Follow Procedures:** Procedures enable others to understand how the work is to be performed through written descriptions of the work activities.

4. **Assign Responsibility:** Make certain that anyone involved with the revised work process understands how to perform his or her work activity and knows what steps to take to ensure that the work process is consistently producing a quality product or service.

Figure 2-18

ACTION 5B:

Determine if the solutions will be effective elsewhere.

The final action in the problem-solving steps requires thinking beyond the current situation and considering where else the solution(s) might be effective. Other workers might want to take advantage of what you have done, thus multiplying the positive impact of your problem-solving activities. The tools for quality improvement you have used will provide clear documentation that others can use to determine if your solution will work for them.

Occasionally, your solution cannot be repeated due to varied circumstances. But at other times, there is potential for a direct application of your work that will result in additional quality improvement. Provide the person who has final approval of your solutions with a list of potential users of your work. This list can be generated by using *BRAINSTORMING.*

Patience Instead Of Fire-fighting

Now that you have gone through each of the problem-solving steps in detail, you are probably ready to attack a problem with what you know. This is understandable; after all, you have been exposed to a process for correcting problems and you want to see it work. It's kind of like buying a new tool or appliance and being anxious to try it out. But just like the new tool or appliance comes with instructions, so do the problem-solving steps.

Apply the problem-solving steps with patience. Don't jump to solutions or be too anxious to move to the next step, because this will keep you in the "fire-fighting" mode. *Fire fighting* is a common symptom of poor quality found at many work locations. It's a two-step dysfunction that works like this:

1. A crisis (problem) arises and a "quick fix" is applied.

2. Then a second crisis arises, and while another "quick fix" is being applied, the first problem flares up again.

Sound familiar? Avoid fire fighting by working carefully through each step of the process. When you do, there will be fewer fires to put out.

Continuous Improvement

In the first chapter I mentioned how using the tools for quality improvement leads to a new way of thinking. This way of thinking is embedded in the problem-solving steps. Problems are confronted by defining them, analyzing the causes, developing alternatives, and standardizing solutions that work to reduce or eliminate them. Once you become skilled in applying the problem-solving steps and tools for quality improvement, problems will no longer seem insurmountable, and quality will become more than just a word.

This new way of thinking goes beyond the application of the problem-solving steps. It requires that you continue to monitor your work processes in order to ensure that customer needs and agreed-upon expectations are met. When customer needs are not met and problems are encountered, you address them by applying the problem-solving steps—as often as necessary.

The problem-solving process is depicted using a *FLOWCHART* in Figure 2-19. The dashed line that returns from Step 5 to Step 1 one represents this new way of thinking. It is a search for excellence; striving for continuous improvement— better and better quality.

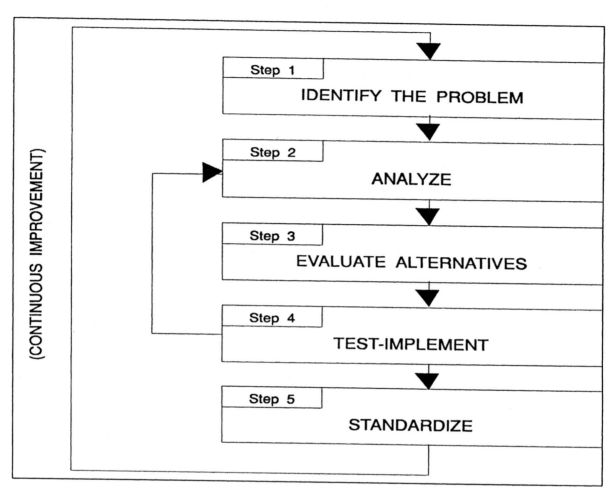

Figure 2-19. Flowchart

In his book *Out of the Crisis*, W. Edwards Deming emphasizes that "At every stage of work there must be continual improvement of methods and procedures, aimed at better satisfaction of the customer (user) at the next stage" (1986, p. 87). We must never become satisfied with our accomplishments. The environment in which we operate demands that we constantly look to improve.

One thing for certain about business today—if you do a good job of staying in one place, you're certain to be run over by the competition. By thinking in terms of continuous improvement, we continue to make progress by striving to improve how well we do things. Continuous improvement is a philosophy of *change*. It accepts change as inevitable, and seeks to get ahead of it by managing its occurrence. In other words, rather than have change occur and then react to it, why not anticipate that change is inevitable and plan for it?

Three

Tools for
Quality Improvement

You have now learned how the tools for quality improvement can be used with a set of problem-solving steps to make beneficial improvements at work and home. In this chapter each of the tools for quality improvement is discussed in detail, so that you can apply them effectively however you choose to use them.

For easy reference, the tools are listed in alphabetical order. The format used to describe each tool is the same. First, a definition is provided, accompanied by a brief description of how the tool can be used. Next, a picture is provided of the tool in its completed form. The intent of these first three items is to provide you with a quick assessment of whether or not a given tool will meet your needs.

Once you have selected a tool as a work aid, follow the step-by-step instructions provided next. You will find that some of the tools are easier to use than others. But the step-by-step instructions will enable you to apply any of the tools for quality improvement easily and correctly.

"Helpful hints" provide additional information that will enable you to use the tools more effectively. The information compiled has been learned through many applications of these tools. Consider the helpful hints as a voice of experience, offered to help you apply the tools correctly so that you can avoid making the same mistakes others have made along the way.

As to the selection of tools, all of the tools included can be used by anyone. There are other tools, of course. Most notable, probably, is the control chart. This tool and others like it (e.g., scatter diagram, failure mode effect analysis (FMEA), design of experiments, quality function deployment (QFD), etc.) were not included because they require a deeper understanding of mathematics than is required for this text. You may desire to increase your knowledge base by learning these tools, but for the vast majority of situations you will encounter, the tools provided here will be more than adequate to meet your needs.

BAR CHART

Definition
A bar chart uses a set of bars to compare the sizes, quantities, amounts, proportions, etc., of related items.

Use
Bar charts are used to break something down into its component parts, to show trends and make comparisons between the items represented by the bars.

Example
In the example of Figure 3-1, a bar chart is used to compare the volume of first quarter sales between four divisions within a company.

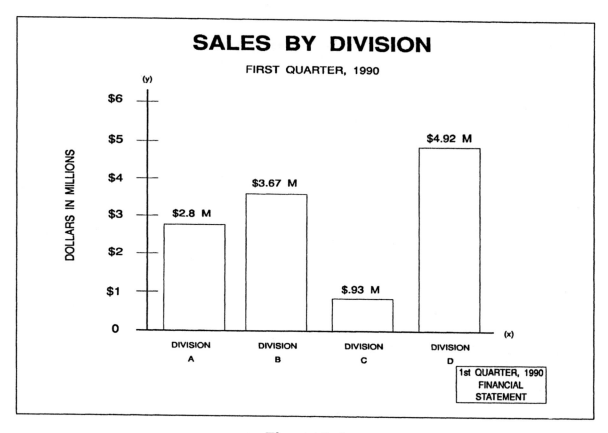

Figure 3-1

Step-by-step Instructions

1.   Select from the three types of bar charts described here the type that best emphasizes what you want to communicate. Two types of bar charts that

BAR CHART

can be used in addition to the simple bar chart shown in the previous example are

- the *clustered* bar chart, and
- the *stratified* bar chart.

In the example of Figure 3-2 a *clustered* bar chart is shown. This chart takes the first quarter sales data presented in the previous example and breaks it down further by type of sale (residential, industrial, foreign) for each division. The sets of bars in a clustered bar chart are always clustered (grouped) without spaces between them; spaces are left only between each major item being compared—in this example, in each division.

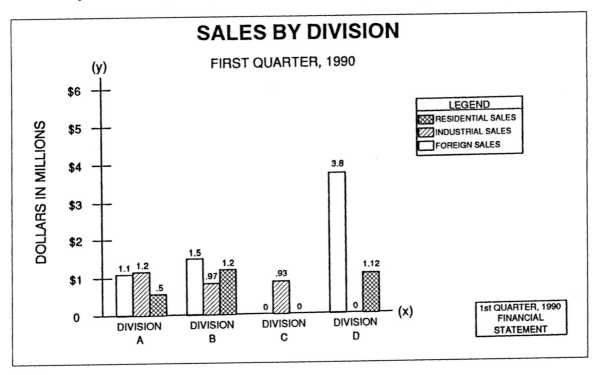

Figure 3-2

Another way to communicate the composition of bars in a bar chart is by using a *stratified* bar chart. The stratified bar chart subdivides each bar horizontally by using color or shading to present the proportional elements that comprise the bar. In the example of Figure 3-3 division sales are again shown as being comprised of residential, industrial, and foreign sales.

2.   Determine how many items (e.g., divisions, products, markets, etc.) are to be compared in the bar chart. The number of items (bars) to be compared determines the length of the horizontal baseline (or x-axis).

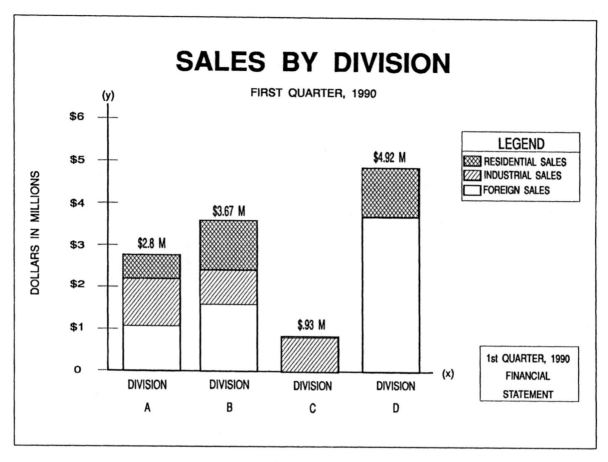

Figure 3-3

3. Choose a scale for the vertical line (or y-axis) that results in it being at least one-third taller than the tallest bar. This avoids giving an impression that the data are filling a required space.

4. Draw bars of equal width for each item, using the scale on the y-axis to determine the height for each bar. Leave equal spaces between the bars or clusters of bars.

5. Label the bar chart. Include source information, sample size, time periods of the measurements, and other helpful information to clarify how the bar chart was constructed.

Helpful hints

1. Remember that the bar chart communicates a message. Decisions you make concerning the items to be compared, and whether to subdivide them, all affect the ability of others to interpret it.

BAR CHART

2.   If the bar chart is being used to emphasize one particular item, and that item is not the largest bar in the set of bars, make sure to highlight it in some way, either by cross hatching, shading, or with a circle around the bar.

3.   Because the relative sizes of similar items are being compared in a bar chart, the bars must be of equal width. Also, keep in mind that wide bars give an impression of strength, and narrow bars give an impression of weakness.

4.   Occasionally, the bar chart is constructed with the x-axis reflecting time-based measurements (e.g., quarters, years). Although there are a few acceptable reasons for doing this, the line graph is better suited to this purpose.

BARRIERS & AIDS

Definition
Barriers & Aids is an analysis and planning technique that identifies obstructing and helping forces.

Use
Barriers & Aids is used to analyze the impact of a proposed change. It also helps in developing plans to make implementing the change easier. By using Barriers & Aids:

- forces are identified that represent barriers to the implementation of a proposed change,

- forces are identified that may aid in the implementation of a proposed change, and

- actions are developed that can counter the influence of barriers to the proposed change.

Example
In the example of Figure 3-4 Barriers & Aids is used to develop lists of hindering and helping forces that might influence the scheduling of a proposed training class for machine operators.

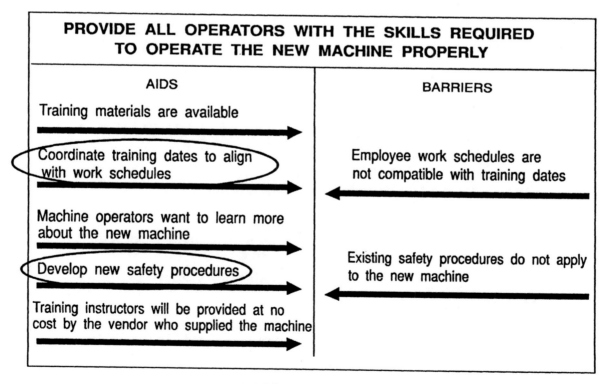

Figure 3-4

BARRIERS & AIDS

Step-by-step instructions

1.   Think through the proposed change. Consider who will be involved in the implementation, and learn all you can about the effect it will have on the existing situation.

2.   Draw a "T" (see Figure 3-5). On top of the "T" write the goal or change to be implemented. Below the top line, on either side of the vertical dividing line, put the words, *Barriers* and *Aids*.

```
+-----------------------------------------------------------+
|           (DESCRIBE WHAT IS DESIRED HERE)                 |
|         _____          |
|                            |                              |
|         BARRIERS           |          AIDS                |
|                            |                              |
|                            |                              |
|                            |                              |
|                            |                              |
|                            |                              |
|                            |                              |
+-----------------------------------------------------------+
```

Figure 3-5

3.   *Brainstorm* (see *BRAINSTORMING*, this chapter) a list of forces that will hinder the implementation of the proposed change. List each hindering force under the word *Barriers*. Every idea listed should have an arrow drawn under it pointing to the right. The arrow symbolizes the force created by the barrier.

4.   *Brainstorm* a list of forces that will help implement the proposed change. List each positive force under the word *Aids*. Every idea listed should have an arrow drawn under it pointing to the left. The arrow symbolizes a force that opposes the barriers.

5.   Evaluate each barrier individually. Then ensure that aids are present to counter the negative force created by each barrier. If necessary, *brainstorm* additional aids for this purpose. Include these new aids with the others, and put a circle around them to signify their importance.

BARRIERS & AIDS

Helpful hints

1. The forces representing barriers and aids can be anything—supplies, equipment, people, money, environment, etc. Be specific in describing how the force will influence the planned change.

2. Sometimes it is useful to assign a weight to each barrier and aid. This action directs attention to the most powerful forces and helps establish a priority for actions identified by the analysis.

3. It is not unusual to think of barriers while attempting to brainstorm aids, and vice versa. When such a thought occurs, don't lose the idea. Have the contributor write it down and then continue the brainstorming session as planned.

BRAINSTORMING

BRAINSTORMING

Definition
Brainstorming is a method for generating and collecting ideas about a given subject from the people who are most familiar with it in the workplace, office, etc.

Use
Brainstorming is used to obtain important information about a subject or process. Brainstorming is also used to enlist participation and generate enthusiasm in a group.

Example
The example of Figure 3-6 is from a brainstorming session on ideas for reducing overtime.

WAYS TO REDUCE OVERTIME

- Increase the number of personnel

- Rearrange the flow of activities in the work for increased efficiency

- Change work assignments to spread the work more equitably among all employees

- Identify causes of rework and reduce or eliminate them using the problem-solving steps

- Train people to accomplish their work efficiently

- Prioritize work asignments so that the most important work gets done first

- Don't commit to completion dates before verifying that they can be achieved

- Require a manager's approval for all overtime worked

- Communicate the need to reduce overtime to all employees and seek to implement their suggestions for improvement where applicable

---

Figure 3-6

Step-by-step instructions

1.   Clarify what is to be brainstormed. The subject can be anything: problems, solutions, procedures, scheduling, etc.

2.   Identify the person responsible for recording the ideas of those involved in the brainstorming session. To help stimulate thinking and generate additional ideas for the list, it is useful to make the list visible to everyone involved.

BRAINSTORMING

3.   Make sure everyone knows how the brainstorming session is to be conducted. There are three approaches commonly used in brainstorming sessions: *one-at-a-time, open door*, and *write-it-down*.

One-at-a-time brainstorming provides everyone with an opportunity to contribute. The session begins with a member of the group offering one idea and continues in the same manner until everyone has a had chance to add to the list. The person responsible for writing the list is also eligible to participate. One-at-a-time brainstorming is a good approach to use when the group involved has many ideas.

Open Door brainstorming involves announcing a subject and then allowing anyone who has a contribution to speak whenever he or she wants. It is useful for stimulating a group, especially when those involved are running out of ideas. It is also useful for starting a brainstorming session when the participants have not used brainstorming before.

Write-it-down brainstorming sessions are used when *confidentiality* is an issue, or when ideas about *several subjects* are to be brainstormed at the same time. The write-it-down approach gives each person involved an opportunity to participate. Ideas are written down rather than stated out loud, but everyone must be able to see each idea listed in order to stimulate thinking.

When *confidentiality* is an issue, ideas are written down by each person individually. They are then collected and accumulated on a list that is shown to the group. This done, additional ideas are invited and collected in the same manner as before.

When the brainstorming session involves *several subjects,* write each subject on a sheet of paper and post it. Everyone involved then passes by each subject sheet, listing ideas as he or she moves along. More than one idea can be posted at a time. Three passes by each sheet is usually sufficient.

4.   When all of the ideas from the brainstorming session are listed, review the list for clarification, making sure that everyone understands each item. This is not a time to criticize ideas, rather it is a time to explain what is meant by an idea if some confusion exists. Reviewing the list also helps to organize it by eliminating duplications and removing ideas that the group feels are no longer applicable.

BRAINSTORMING

Helpful hints

1. The following are some basic *rules of order* that should be followed during a brainstorming session:

    a. Criticizing and evaluating ideas are not permitted.

    b. Reinforce and encourage creative ideas.

    c. Build on the ideas of others.

    d. Passing is allowed if you don't have an idea to contribute, or if someone has taken the idea you had. Passing doesn't mean losing your turn the next time around in a one-at-a-time session.

2. Concentrate on getting as many ideas as possible, as quickly as possible.

3. The person responsible for preparing the list, sometimes called the scribe, should develop a clear, legible list of ideas that can be easily read during the session and later. The scribe should write down ideas as they are given and ensure that each idea is understandable. The scribe should not edit an idea without the approval of the person submitting it.

4. Identify "off limit areas" before beginning a brainstorming session. For example, if the subject to be brainstormed is *"Ways of Handling Overtime Staffing Requirements,"* an idea for changing a collective bargaining agreement would most likely be off limits.

CAUSE-AND-EFFECT DIAGRAM

Definition
Cause-and-effect analysis identifies the factors (causes) that lead to an outcome (effect).

Use
Cause-and-effect analysis employs a *fishbone diagram* to separate and identify the root causes of a problem when many causes exist.

Example
In Figure 3-7, causes are identified for the problem, *"Johnny has been late for his first class eight times during the past three months."* Root causes have been circled.

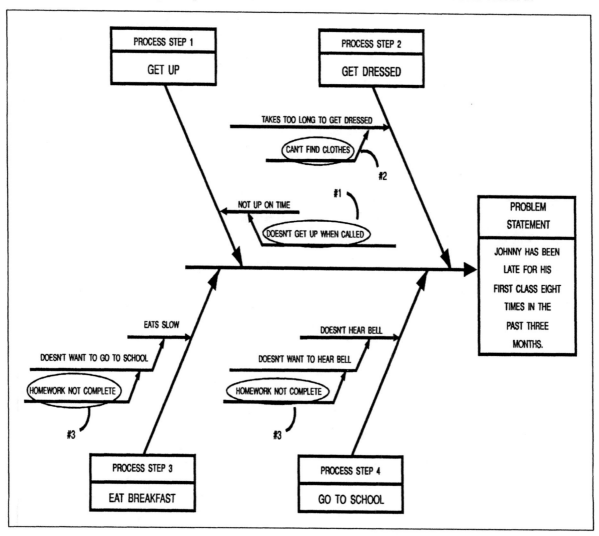

Figure 3-7

CAUSE-AND-EFFECT DIAGRAM

Step-by-step instructions

1.   Before cause-and-effect analysis can begin, a clear statement of an effect (problem) must be developed and supported with data.

2.   Begin construction of the fishbone diagram by placing the effect (problem) in a box on the right. Next, draw a horizontal arrow leading into the effect (problem) box. See Figure 3-8.

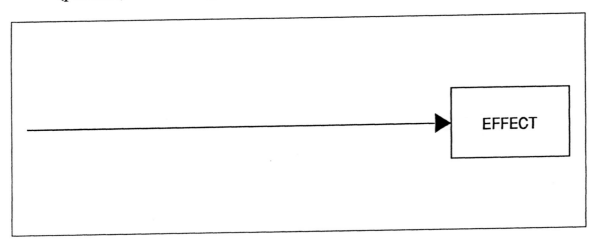

Figure 3-8

3.   Identify three to six major bones. The major bones can be identified using one of these three alternatives:

    a. When a recognizable process, or repetitive set of activities, results in the effect (problem) being analyzed, the major steps in the process can be used as the major bones in the fishbone diagram.

    b. The major bones can be assigned the titles of People, Materials, Machines, and Methods. These four areas include the broad range of causes that produce most effects (problems).

    c. Labels for the major bones can be developed by *BRAINSTORMING* a list of all the factors that cause the effect to occur. After the brainstorm list is developed, review it and group together the causes that relate to one another. Label each group of causes and use these labels for the major bones.

4.   Draw the major "bones" as slanting arrows leading into the center arrow. If you want to convey a sense of order to the major bones, such as the major steps in a process, alternate the arrows above and below the center

arrow to reflect these steps, starting with the first bone at the left. See Figure 3-9.

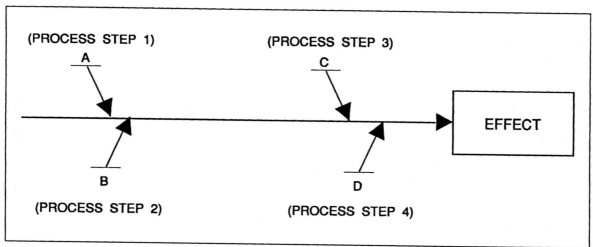

Figure 3-9

5. Identify *first-level* causes related to each major bone. These causes are identified by *brainstorming* responses to the question, "How does this major bone cause the effect under investigation to occur?" List each identified cause, using an arrow pointing to a major bone. See Figure 3-10.

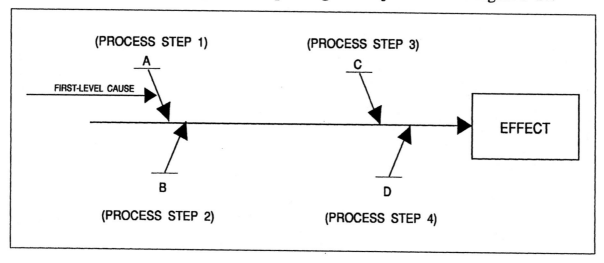

Figure 3-10

CAUSE-AND-EFFECT DIAGRAM

6.   Identify *second-level* causes for each first-level cause. Second-level causes are identified by *brainstorming* responses to the question, "What causes this (first-level cause) to occur?" List each second-level cause on an arrow attached to the first-level cause. There may be more than one second-level cause for each first-level cause. See Figure 3-11.

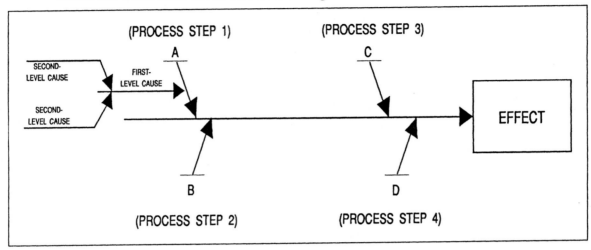

Figure 3-11

7.   Identify *third-level* causes related to each second-level cause. Third-level causes are identified by *brainstorming* responses to the question, "What causes this (second-level cause) to occur?" List each third-level cause on an arrow attached to the second-level cause. There may be more than one third-level cause for each second-level cause. See Figure 3-12.

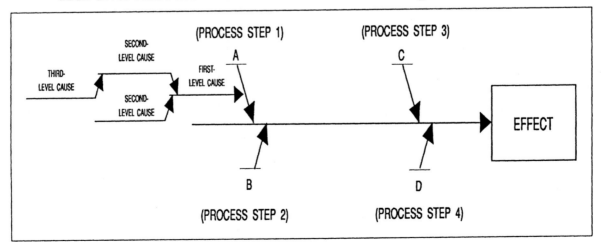

Figure 3-12

CAUSE-AND-EFFECT DIAGRAM

8. Continue in the same manner, identifying *fourth-* and *fifth-level* causes where they exist. When additional causes cannot be identified, move to Step 9.

9. Check for continuity by reviewing the entire fishbone diagram, beginning with the highest-level causes (fifth, fourth, third, second, then first). Complete this check by asking, "Does this (third-level cause) cause this (second-level cause) to occur?" You should be able to answer yes at each level, all the way to the effect (problem) listed in the box on the right. When problems with continuity are identified, rework the cause-and-effect relationships using the instructions in Step 6 or 7.

10. Identify potential root causes. Select causes that occur more than once, or appear to have a significant impact on the effect (problem). Highlight these causes by putting a circle around them. See Figure 3-13.

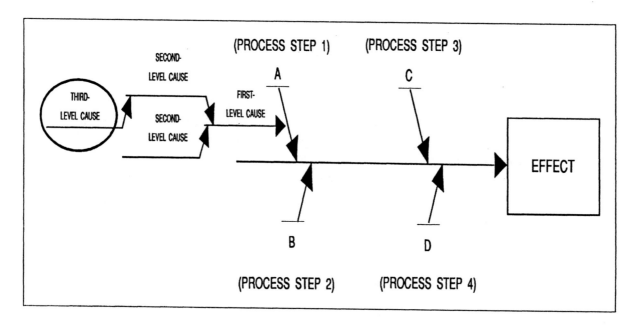

Figure 3-13

11. Verify each potential root cause. Analyze the data available, or gather additional data to make certain your assumptions are correct. Cause-and-effect analysis is a process that begins with experience-based guesses and progresses toward data-based analysis. Add data to the fishbone diagram to support your conclusions.

CAUSE-AND-EFFECT DIAGRAM

In the example of Figure 3-14 the identified root cause can be proven responsible for 30% of the effect (problem) listed in the box on the right.

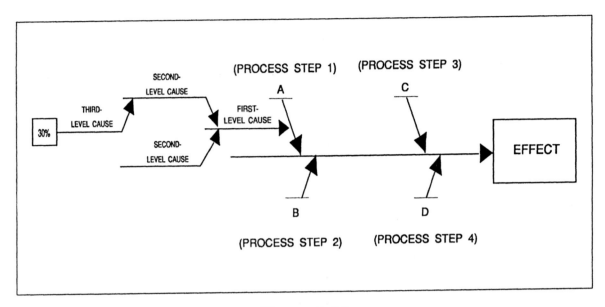

Figure 3-14

Helpful hints

1.   Simplify the fishbone diagram when presenting it to others. This helps them understand your analysis by removing distractions and focusing their attention on important cause-and-effect relationships. Simplifying the fishbone diagram is accomplished by removing everything except the major bones and the detail that has linkage to the root causes. All other causes are not presented, but remain available for reference.

2.   Cause-and-effect analysis should present a *clear* understanding of the causal relationships that contribute to a problem. When a fishbone diagram becomes too complex to understand, break it up into several fishbone diagrams—one for each major bone, for example.

3.   How deep should the analysis go? The simple answer is, "Enough to work from the effect (problem) back to the root causes." A common rule of thumb is to ask the question, "What causes this to occur?" at least five times. Don't settle on a potential root cause too quickly, and don't go beyond what is humanly possible to address. True root causes are those that can be acted upon to achieve the desired end.

4.   The only way to confirm the identification of a root cause is to reduce or remove it from the actual work environment and see if the effect (problem)

CAUSE-AND-EFFECT DIAGRAM

shows a corresponding change. To accomplish this, test-implement solutions selected to reduce or eliminate a suspected root cause. Then monitor every solution implemented. When a permanent change in the effect (problem) is observed, a root cause has been identified.

For example, suppose *machine failures* is a suspected root cause of the effect (problem), *"Typing errors have increased by 50%."* A team of employees selects several solutions and test-implements them to eliminate the machine failures. Each solution is monitored to establish how much it contributes to the reduction in typing errors. When a permanent reduction in typing errors can be linked to an implemented solution, a root cause has been identified.

5.   Cause-and-effect analysis takes time, patience, and investigative endurance. Although there are certain rules to follow, the success of the technique depends to a high degree on the ingenuity and persistence of those doing the analysis.

CHECKSHEET

CHECKSHEET

Definition
The checksheet is a simple but powerful data-gathering tool.

Use
A checksheet is used to gather and classify information (data). Effective checksheets collect data that can be easily analyzed to identify patterns in the work being studied.

Example
In Figure 3-15 a checksheet is used to collect information about machine breakdowns that occur over a one-week period. This example assumes that the cause of each breakdown is being tracked elsewhere.

DAILY BREAKDOWN SHEET

FREQUENCY ITEM	MON 2/24/90	TUE 2/25/90	WED 2/26/90	THU 2/27/90	FRI 2/28/90	TOTAL
MACHINE 1 (RJ 706)	✓✓✓		✓✓			5
MACHINE 2 (RB 403)		✓				1
MACHINE 3 (RT 955)	✓			✓✓		3
TOTAL	4	1	2	2	0	9

BETA PLANT
DETERGENT LINE

Figure 3-15

Step-by-step Instructions

1   Establish what is to be monitored. Think about the information you will need to analyze the area under investigation. In the previous example, the number of machine breakdowns is being monitored.

2.   Once you have identified what is to be monitored, plan to gather all necessary and useful information. In the previous example, a checksheet is used to compare all similar machines.

CHECKSHEET

3. Establish time periods for gathering the data. Decide how often to record the information (e.g., hourly, daily, weekly, etc.).

4. Construct a checksheet to record the data you have decided to collect. The size of a checksheet is determined by the amount of information that needs to be gathered. Put the items to be monitored on the left and the time periods across the top. Always arrange the checksheet with the subject information on the left, and the observation periods on the right. See Figure 3-16.

DAILY BREAKDOWN SHEET

	MON	TUE	WED	THU	FRI	TOTAL
MACHINE 1						
MACHINE 2						
MACHINE 3						
TOTAL						

Figure 3-16

5. Provide space for totals on the right for each item being observed and along the bottom for the observation periods. This will help with calculations, and the documentation of information from the observation period. See Figure 3-17.

DAILY BREAKDOWN SHEET

	MON	TUE	WED	THU	FRI	TOTAL
MACHINE 1	✓✓✓		✓✓			5
MACHINE 2		✓				1
MACHINE 3	✓			✓✓		3
TOTAL	4	1	2	2	0	9

Figure 3-17

CHECKSHEET

6.   Keep track of when the data gathering began, when it stopped, where it occurred, who collected the information, and how it was collected.

7.   Label the checksheet clearly. Include a source legend with information that further defines the data represented.

Helpful hints

1.   The best way to arrange a checksheet is the one that makes gathering and interpreting the information easiest.

2.   Data must be collected the same way each time they are recorded to ensure consistency and accuracy. Make sure everyone involved understands exactly when and how the information is to be collected or the measurement is to be taken.

3.   Label everything on the checksheet carefully. When there is more than one person using a checksheet, someone may forget exactly what must be entered or when it is to be entered. Incorrect entries will reduce or destroy the value of the information collected.

      For example, if you are interested in the number of breakdowns occurring on three different machines, ensure that everyone using the checksheet knows which is machine #1, #2 and #3. Also, be precise in gathering the data. Instead of "Monday," describe the information collected precisely: "Monday, 2/24/90." See Figure 3-18.

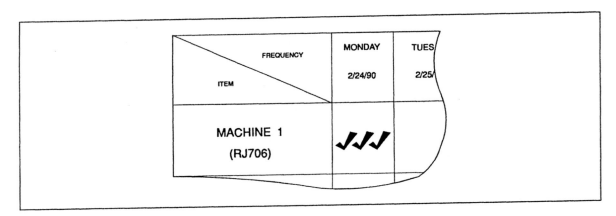

Figure 3-18

5.   Plan carefully to gather enough but not too much information. Gathering too little information will cause frustration and delays in completing the analysis. Gathering more information than necessary will be time- and labor-intensive.

FLOWCHART

Definition
A flowchart is a graphic illustration of the activities in a process.

Use
The flowchart is used to clarify a process by documenting the activities involved and their sequence. A flowchart enables everyone involved in the process to understand how his or her work contributes to the product or service produced. Flowcharts are also used to improve processes. Flowcharts highlight inefficiencies, along with missing, repetitive, or unnecessary steps.

Example
The example of Figure 3-19 is a flowchart of the activities involved in handling customer telephone inquiries.

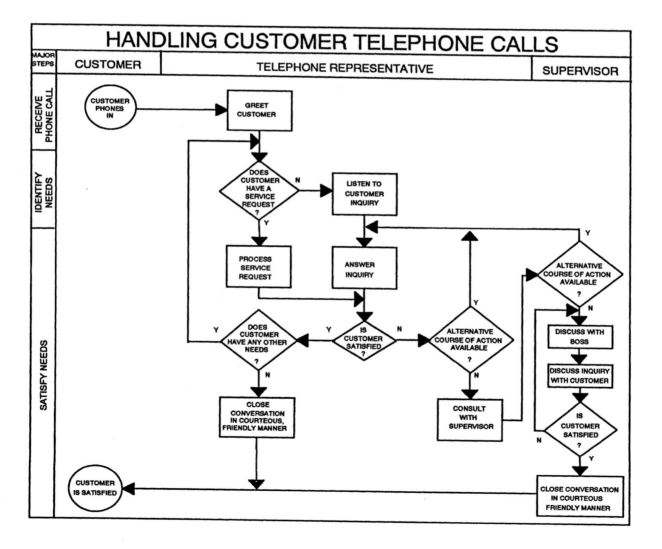

Figure 3-19

FLOWCHART

Step-by-step instructions

1.   Establish the level of detail the flowchart is to represent. Flowcharts can be used to document the activities in a process at any level. Higher-level flow charts leave out the detailed activities in a process. In Figure 3-19, for instance, the activity *"Process Service Request"* probably involves several tasks. Although they are not listed here, they might be on a lower-level flowchart. The level of detail you select will depend on the purpose for constructing the flowchart.

2.   Title the process to be charted. In our example, the title is "Handling Customer Telephone Calls."

3.   Identify the major steps in the process. To do this, list all of the activities to be included in the flowchart, then review the list to identify the major steps involved. An alternative is to use *Plan, Do, Check,* and *Act* as the major steps. These broad-based actions are present in most processes. Once the major steps are identified, list them on the left side of the chart.

4.   Under the name of the flowchart list the names of the people, departments, etc., that are responsible for the process activities to be included in the flowchart. See Figure 3-20.

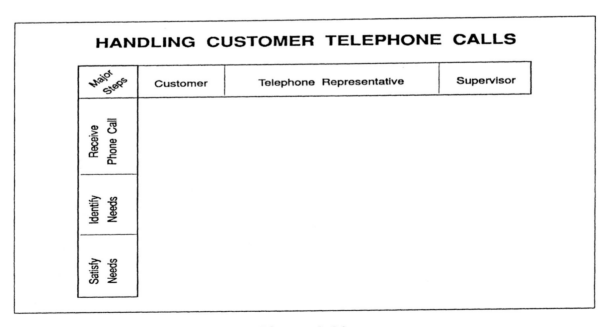

Figure 3-20

FLOWCHART

5.   Place the activities to be included under the appropriate person, department or organization and next to the corresponding major step. Use the symbols in Figure 3-21 to clarify each activity.

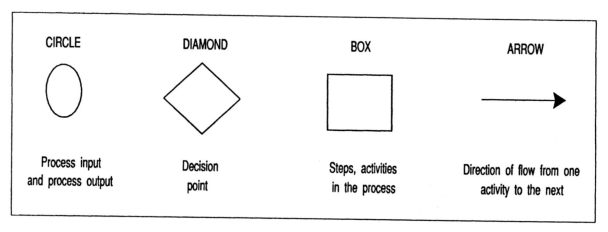

Figure 3-21

Helpful hints

1.   When preparing a flowchart for the first time, attempt to identify the activities currently used each time the process is performed. These activities can vary, especially with a process that has not been formally documented before. It may be difficult to separate activities "being used" from activities that "should be used." When this occurs, begin by creating a flowchart of "what is" and then create another flowchart of "what should be." The two flowcharts will serve to document any changes made to the process and will assist in understanding their effects on the process output.

2.   Plan to revise the flowchart as you learn more about the process. After a process is documented in a flowchart, pass the flowchart around to those who work with the process. Ask for their input. Use what they say to make adjustments and clarifications.

3.   For the sake of clarity, make sure the flowchart has no more than one arrow going in and one arrow coming out of each circle or box. At decision points, the diamond should have no more than one arrow going in and two arrows coming out—one labeled "Yes" and the other labeled "No."

HISTOGRAM

HISTOGRAM

Definition
A histogram illustrates the frequency with which related things or events occur.

Use
Histograms are used to improve processes, products, and services by identifying patterns of occurrence.

Example
In the example of Figure 3-22, a histogram is used to display the time required to complete 50 different phone conversations. Several interesting facts can be observed in the histogram:

- No call took less than 3 minutes and no call took 8 minutes or more.

- The average phone call took 4.9 minutes.

- Most of the phone calls took between 3.65 and 5.75 minutes.

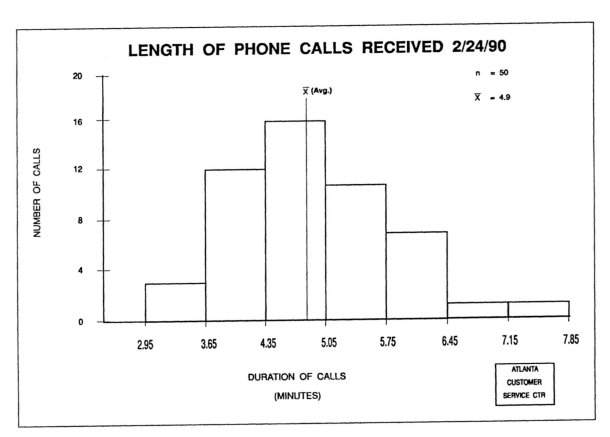

Figure 3-22

Step-by-step Instructions

1. Gather at least 50 data points. Histograms are constructed to create a picture from the data collected. If the picture is to be accurate and meaningful, sufficient data must be obtained. (In Figure 3-22 the number of data points is indicated by n = 50.)

2. Calculate the *range* of the data points by subtracting the lowest data point from the highest. In Figure 3-23, the 50 data points used in the "phone call" example are provided. Of all the numbers 7.8 is the highest and 3.0 is the lowest. The difference between these numbers, or the range, is 4.8—which for our purposes can be rounded to 5.

LENGTH OF PHONE CALLS RECEIVED ON 2/24/90 (in minutes)									
4.4	5.0	4.5	6.3	4.0	3.8	4.1	3.5	4.3	6.4
4.3	3.7	4.8	3.2	5.9	4.6	3.7	4.2	4.9	5.4
4.0	5.7	4.9	3.8	5.6	5.3	4.0	4.8	3.0	4.7
5.6	7.8	5.5	6.5	4.9	4.5	5.6	5.6	5.7	3.9
6.2	6.1	5.7	4.7	4.5	5.0	4.7	6.3	5.2	4.2

Figure 3-23

3. Calculate the *number of bars* to be used in the histogram. A simple way to do this is to take the square root of the number of data points. In the phone call example there are 50 data points. The square root of 50 is 7.07. This number is also rounded off, so that seven bars will be constructed.

4. Determine how *wide* each bar will be. To do this, divide the range by the number of bars to be constructed. In our example the range is 5 and the number of bars to be constructed is 7. 5÷7 = .71 To make this number easier to work with, it is rounded off to .7, making each bar .7 minutes wide.

5. Calculate the interval or vertical *boundary* lines for each bar. This is the most complicated step in the construction of a histogram, but one that can be easily performed if you follow actions a, b, and c, which follow.

    An incorrect, but seemingly logical method of calculating interval boundaries is to begin with the lowest data point (in our example 3) and

HISTOGRAM

add .7 (the width calculated for each bar). Thus, 3 + .7 = 3.7; this results in boundaries for the first bar of 3 and 3.7. But note the problem with this approach. Two of the fifty phone calls lasted 3.7 minutes. If the boundary between the first and second bar is 3.7, then neither bar can include the two 3.7-minute data points.

To avoid this problem, the histogram must be constructed so that each measurement in the data set falls within a bar and not on a boundary line. This means that the number assigned to the boundaries for each bar must be different from the numbers in the data set. Calculating these boundary numbers is explained in a, b, and c:

a. Identify the most *refined number* in the data set and develop numbers that are one decimal more refined than that. A refined number is more detailed or specific than other numbers. In the phone call example, all numbers having one digit following the decimal point are equally refined, providing many "most refined numbers." Therefore, in this example, any number with two digits behind the decimal point will be more refined than any number in the data set.

b. Calculate the interval or boundaries for the first bar. Start by developing the lower boundary number for the first bar. To accomplish this, identify the lowest data point and subtract a number from it to create a boundary number that is more refined than the most refined number. In the example, the lowest data point is 3. By subtracting .05 from it a number is developed that is more refined than the most refined number in the data set: 3 - .05 = 2.95. In this example .05 was used to make the calculation easy. Any number that has two or more digits behind the decimal point could have been used to develop the refined number.

The second or higher boundary number for the first bar is calculated by adding the width of each bar to the first boundary number. In the example, .7 is the width established for each bar (from steps 3 and 4), so the second boundary for the first bar is calculated by adding .7 to 2.95: 2.95 + .7 = 3.65. Therefore, the boundaries for the first bar are 2.95 and 3.65.

c. Calculate the boundaries for the other bars in the histogram. This is accomplished by adding the width of each bar to the second boundary number for the bar preceding it. (This means that the second boundary number for each bar is also the first boundary number for the next bar. Put another way, there will be no spaces between bars.)

In the phone call example, the first bar has boundaries of 2.95 and 3.65. The second bar will have boundaries of 3.65 and 3.65 + .7, or 4.35.

Continue in the same manner until the boundary numbers for all the bars are calculated.

6.   Construct a frequency table. A frequency table organizes the data points from lowest to highest in accordance with the boundaries established for each bar. Construct the frequency table as shown in Figure 3-24 with the boundary numbers listed in a column on the left and the data points on the right. Include totals to aid in checking your work.

LENGTH OF PHONE CALLS RECEIVED 2/24/90

LENGTH OF CALLS (MINUTES)	FREQUENCY	TOTAL
2.95 — 3.65	✓✓✓	3
3.65 — 4.35	✓✓✓✓✓✓✓✓✓✓✓✓	12
4.35 — 5.05	✓✓✓✓✓✓✓✓✓✓✓✓✓✓✓✓	16
5.05 — 5.75	✓✓✓✓✓✓✓✓✓✓✓	11
5.75 — 6.45	✓✓✓✓✓✓	6
6.45 — 7.15	✓	1
7.15 — 7.85	✓	1
	TOTAL	50

ATLANTA CUSTOMER SERV. CTR

Figure 3-24

7.   Begin construction of the histogram by placing the boundary numbers for each bar on a horizontal line with zero at the left end. Next, draw a vertical scale from zero and high enough to include the bar with the greatest number of data points.

8.   Plot the data points and draw in the bars of the histogram. A bar is constructed for each group of data points. There should be no spaces between bars, and the height of each bar is equal to the number of data points in that bar. If there are no data points between certain boundaries, then no bar is drawn. See Figure 3-25.

HISTOGRAM

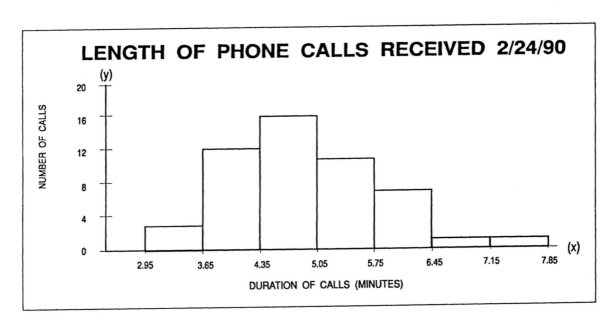

Figure 3-25

9.   Complete the histogram by listing the number of data points, and calculating their average ($\overline{X}$). In the phone call example, the number of data points is 50 (n = 50). To calculate the average, add them up and divide by the number of data points. In the phone call example, the sum of the data points equals 245.0, and the number of data points is 50.

245 ÷ 50 = 4.9 Therefore, the average phone call ($\overline{X}$) is 4.9 minutes.

10.   As with all charts and graphs, clear titles should be included, along with a source box describing where the data were obtained.

Helpful hints

1.   The clearest histograms have no fewer than five and no more than twelve bars. Fewer than five bars does not provide enough detail; more than twelve bars is too crowded and difficult to construct.

2.   Once the histogram has been constructed, the following information will help interpret the pictures obtained from the data.

a. *Normal Histogram:* Histograms like the one in Figure 3-22 are what most histograms will look like once you have constructed them. *Action required:* None. Use the histogram to understand the process that produced the data presented.

b. *Bimodal histogram:* A histogram like Figure 3-26 usually indicates that there are two types of data under observation. In other words, the picture is not clear because two different things are being considered. An example might be a histogram with the heights of both men and women mixed together. Because the average height of men is taller than the average height of women, a histogram with two "mountains" is created. *Action required:* Clarify the situation by further classifying the data and creating two histograms.

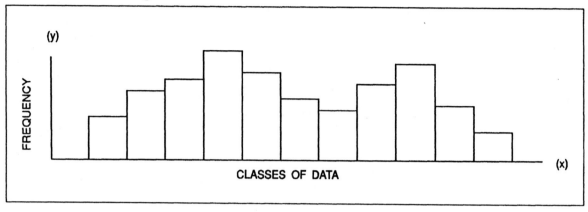

Figure 3-26

c. *Broken Tooth or "Comb" Histogram*: A histogram like the one in Figure 3-27 usually indicates that it has been constructed improperly. *Action required:* Recalculate and redraw the histogram.

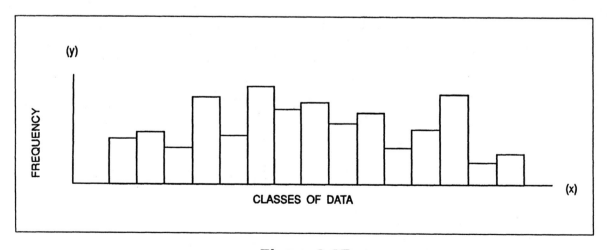

Figure 3-27

HISTOGRAM

d. *Cut-Off Histogram:* A histogram with this configuration of bars, or one similar to it with all high bars to one side (Figure 3-28), indicates that some data have been excluded from consideration. Possible reasons for this include 100% inspection eliminating some of the data points (even though the remaining dispersion can still be reduced), or certain data values being unable to occur; values less than a certain number may not be possible. *Action required:* No action necessary if there is a good reason for the histogram to look this way. Find the reason. Check your calculations. Collect more data if necessary.

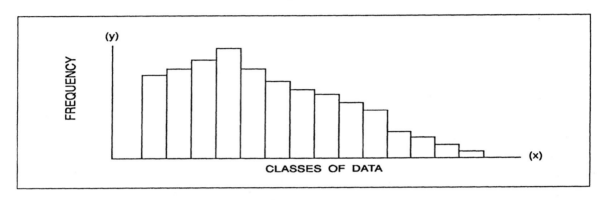

Figure 3-28

e. *Skewed Histogram:* The histogram in Figure 3-29 has most of the data located at one end (it could occur at either end) of the x-axis rather than centering around the average. It's also not unusual in skewed histograms to have "outliers" or data points well isolated from the other bars of the histogram. *Action required:* Check to make sure the outliers are not due to an error in calculation or measurement. If they are legitimate, investigate them for cause using the problem-solving steps. Also, determine why the data is not centered around the average, and take action if necessary.

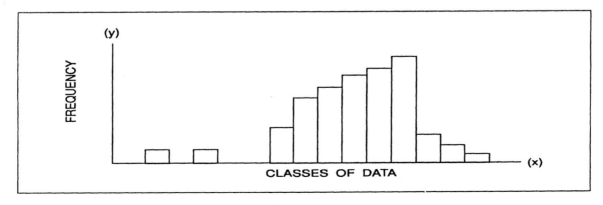

Figure 3-29

INTERVIEW

Definition

An interview is an exchange of information utilizing face-to-face or telephone communication.

Use

The interview can be used to understand and measure customer needs, attitudes, and satisfaction with products and services. It is best applied when the information required is available from a relatively small group of people who can answer questions directly.

Example

Examples of an interview can be seen during any television newscast, as reporters utilize this technique to obtain information from people who are knowledgeable about the subject being reported.

Step-by-step Instructions

1.   Verify that the interview is the best way to collect the information. If the number of people to be interviewed is large, or hard to communicate with directly, the *SURVEY* might be a more appropriate tool.

2.   Set objectives for the interview. Write objectives that clarify what you want to learn from the interview. An objective for an interview might be to *"determine how people will respond to a change in procedures."*

3.   Identify who will be involved with the interview:

   ■ *Those being interviewed: The number of people to be interviewed depends upon the objectives of the interview and who is available. Try to interview people who are recognized authorities in the subject area. Also, interview people who represent a cross-section of others who work with, or are otherwise involved with, the subject area.*

   ■ *Those conducting the interviews:* To reduce variation in the data collected, it is a good idea to limit the number of people who will be conducting the interviews. Select people who are familiar with the objectives of the interview and knowledgeable about the subject being addressed.

4.   Find out what you can about the people who will be interviewed. Determine how they feel about the subject of the interview. Try to do this indirectly by talking with people who know the interviewees. Use the information

INTERVIEW

you gather to develop questions that those being interviewed will respond to easily.

5.   Develop the interview questions. Use questions that meet the objectives of the interview. Usually, the information gathered during an interview can be analyzed more easily if some of the questions require a numerical or objective response. Responses can easily be measured if the potential answers are associated with a scale like that shown in Figure 3-30. Additional easy- to-measure questions call for True/False or Yes/No responses.

Example of an objective question:

To what extent will you tell others about the XYZ product?

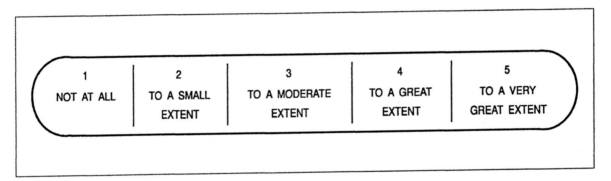

Figure 3-30

6.   Arrange the questions so that the interview flows smoothly. The interview should be conversational, with the questions arranged so that one thought leads logically to the next. Evaluate how well your questions accomplish this by interviewing someone not on the interview list first. Use what you learn from this trial run to modify the interview questions. The trial run is also a good opportunity to see how long it takes to conduct the interview. Modify the interview to meet time constraints and plan to ask the most important questions first in case the interview is cut short.

7.   Make an appointment for the interview. Set up the interview ahead of time by letting the person being interviewed know why the interview is being conducted and how much time will be required.

8.   Conduct the interview. Ask the questions developed to meet your objectives the same way during every interview. Spend most of the interview listening carefully and taking notes. These notes are an important record of the

answers given and contain the data from which conclusions will be drawn later. If you desire to use a tape recorder, gain permission ahead of time.

If you are not sure what was meant by an answer, ask a clarifying question. For example, "Do you mean that . . ." or "Allow me to summarize what I heard you say." If the discussion gets off track, return to the planned questions. Remember to use the time allotted wisely. Complete the interview by thanking the interviewee for his or her time and cooperation.

9.   Review the information obtained. Do this as soon as possible following the interview. The notes taken during an interview are sometimes reduced in value because they are difficult to understand or illegible. Reorganize them if necessary for clarification.

10.   When the interviews are completed, analyze the data collected. Look for trends based on measurable evidence. The interview design will help make this task easy. Use other tools for quality improvement to organize and display the data, for example, the checksheet, Pareto, bar or pie charts.

Helpful hints

1.   If you have never conducted or prepared an interview before, it is a good idea to involve someone who has. Ask such a person to review the interview design. Such a person should be able to offer some useful suggestions.

2.   Interviews can be a burden to the person being interviewed when they are not done well. Make sure your objectives are clear. Develop questions that are relevant to the objectives. Stay on track and listen carefully. Take as many notes as you can.

3.   When true/false or similar questions are asked to obtain measurable data from an interview, be sure to include an open-ended question as a follow-up. This gives the person being interviewed an opportunity to explain his or her answers and will provide you with valuable data for later use. Examples of open-ended questions follow:

      a.   Why do you think so?

      b.   How would you deal with this situation?

      c.   What would you recommend?

LINE GRAPH

LINE GRAPH

Definition
A line graph charts the variation in data over time.

Use
Line graphs are used to display change. They are useful for showing improvement, identifying problems, and communicating trends. Line graphs show progress toward, or deviation from, an established target.

Example
In Figure 3-31 a line graph is used to track the number of late payment notices mailed to customers over a five-year period.

Step-by-step instructions

1.   Identify an existing measure or indicator. Alternatively, you may wish to develop a new one and collect the data with which to monitor it. In Figure 3-31 the measure is the total number of late notices mailed per year.

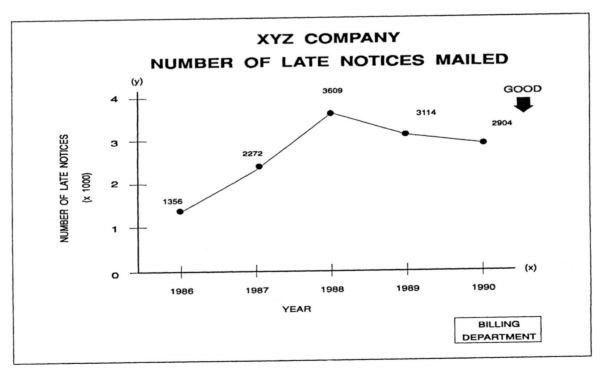

Figure 3-31

LINE GRAPH

2.   Decide how often to take the measurement. Measurements can be taken at any interval—hourly, daily, weekly, monthly, annually, etc. To decide how often to take the measurement, clarify why the measurement is needed. In Figure 3-31 the measurement is taken annually. This annual measurement is useful for communicating major trends, but doesn't reveal much about the work activities that account for the late notices being mailed. To find out why so many late notices are being mailed, the activities that contribute to the annual measurement must be taken at shorter intervals.

3.   Construct a horizontal line (x-axis) to track each measurement obtained. All line graphs are constructed to show time on the x-axis. The x-axis should display a sufficient amount of time to be meaningful. For example, a person looking at Figure 3-31 would have difficulty drawing any conclusions if only one or two years were displayed.

4.   Construct a vertical line (y-axis) to show the frequency or quantity being measured. The y-axis must be at least one-third lower than the lowest data point, and one-third higher than the highest data point. In Figure 3-31, the lowest data point is 1356 and the highest is 3609.

5.   To plot a data point, use the date of the measurement to locate the corresponding time point on the x-axis. Draw a dot on the chart directly above this time point and in line with the number measured on the y-axis.

6.   When more than one point has been posted, connect all dots with a solid line.

7.   To benefit others who are unfamiliar with the information being presented, place an arrow in the upper right-hand corner with the word "good" to indicate which direction is favorable.

Helpful hints

1.   Line graphs are easily abused because of their flexibility. They may be drawn in ways that misrepresent or distort reality. Trends are sometimes buried when the time scale (x-axis) is too infrequent—every quarter, for example, instead of every month. Similarly, y-axis scales with larger intervals tend to flatten the line and not show variation well. Y-axis scales that are too narrow exaggerate the change taking place and may not leave enough room for future data points.

2.   Line graphs can measure practically anything: amounts, weights, depths, heights, etc. Usually, line graphs are used to track the output of a work process. When this is the case use care in selecting a measure that

LINE GRAPH

accurately represents the whole process. For example, to monitor the total time required to get ready for work, you wouldn't want to measure the time it takes to eat breakfast, because eating breakfast is only one of the activities involved in the process for getting ready for work. A better measure would be *walking out the door time minus getting out of bed time*. Of course, if you constructed a line graph of this information and found there was a problem, then you might want to measure the subprocesses involved with getting ready for work—like eating breakfast.

3.   When sharp "spikes" appear in a line graph, research the cause. This might mean a special cause has occurred that requires action. To help others who might look at the graph understand what has happened, note the reason for the spike next to it with a written comment. (See Chapter 4, Figure 4-19.)

4.   It is sometimes useful to track more than one line of data on a line graph to compare trends. (See Chapter 4, Figure 4-26.)

LIST REDUCTION

Definition
List reduction reduces a large list of items to a manageable few.

Use
List reduction is frequently used to decrease the number of items identified during a brainstorming session.

Example
In Figure 3-32 votes have been tallied to reduce a brainstormed list from nine items to three.

A BRAINSTORMED LIST OF KNOWN WAYS TO REDUCE OVERTIME	VOTES PER ITEM
1. Increase the number of personnel	✔
2. Rearrange the flow of activities in the work for increased efficiency	✔✔
3. Change work assignments to spread the work more equitably among all employees	✔✔✔✔
4. Identify causes of rework and reduce or eliminate them by using the problem solving steps	✔✔✔✔✔✔✔
5. Train people to accomplish their work efficiently	✔✔✔✔✔
6. Prioritize work assignments so that the most important work gets done first	✔✔
7. Don't commit to completion dates before verifying that they can be achieved	✔
8. Require a manager's approval for all overtime worked	✔
9. Communicate the need to reduce overtime to all employees and seek to implement their suggestions for improvement where applicable	✔

Figure 3-32

LIST REDUCTION

Step-by-step instructions

1.   Make the list of items to be reduced visible to everyone involved in the list-reduction activity.

2.   Vote for any item on the list. As each listed item is called out by the group leader, anyone who wants to maintain it on the list votes for it. Everyone involved is eligible to vote as many times as they want, but only one vote per person per item. Votes are cast by raising the hand. Encouraging others to vote for an item, or "politicking," is not allowed.

3.   Once the first round of voting is completed, items receiving the largest number of votes are circled. The number of votes required for a circle is agreed to by those people involved in the list-reduction activity. Usually, a group of five to eight people will circle any item receiving three votes or more.

4.   Identify three to five of the "most significant" items. If more than three to five circled items remain on the list after the first round of voting, everyone votes again. In the second round of voting each person is allocated a limited number of votes. The number of votes is determined by dividing the circled items by 2. For example, if the number of circled items is 10, each person is assigned five votes. The assigned votes can be cast for any circled item with no more than one vote per item. Again, votes are cast by raising the hand. No discussion is allowed, except to clarify the meaning of an item.

5.   Continue reducing the list in this manner until no more or less than three to five items remain.

Helpful hints

1.   List reduction is appropriate for reducing a list so that the few items remaining can be discussed and evaluated carefully using another tool for quality improvement—the MATRIX.

2.   Make sure everyone understands the rules of list reduction before the voting begins and then work quickly to reduce the list.

3.   Discussion of the items should be limited to clarification only. If the list was generated using brainstorming, each item should have already been clarified, and like items combined or eliminated as appropriate.

MATRIX

Definition

A matrix is a grid of intersecting horizontal and vertical lines.

Use

The matrix is used to evaluate and define the strength of the relationship that exists between a set of options and a set of criteria. The matrix is useful for selecting one option from a brainstormed list that has already been reduced by list reduction.

Example

In Figure 3-33 a matrix is used to evaluate and select one problem from four that are under consideration.

PROBLEM-SELECTION MATRIX

PROBLEMS UNDER CONSIDERATION	EVALUATION CRITERIA				TOTAL
	IMPACT ON THE CUSTOMER	RELATIONSHIP TO BUSINESS OBJECTIVES	NEED FOR IMPROVEMENT	RESOURCES REQUIRED	
1. Equipment not properly installed	1	1	1	2	5
2. Operators not trained	2	1	3	1	7
3. Not enough time to comply with operating standards	2	1	3	2	8
4. Work space too cluttered	1	1	3	1	6

OPTIONS

LEGEND: 3 = HIGH   2 = MEDIUM   1 = LOW

Figure 3-33

MATRIX

Step-by-step Instructions

1.   Identify the choices or options to be evaluated.

2.   Identify criteria for evaluating the selected options. For example, if you were getting a car painted, the following criteria might be selected:

- the quality of paint to be used

- the number of coats that will be applied

- whether or not a warranty is offered

- how well other customers are satisfied with the work of the paint shop

3.   Construct a two-sided matrix and post the evaluation criteria across the top and the options under consideration along the side. Include a "Total" column across from the options. See Figure 3-34.

PROBLEMS UNDER CONSIDERATION	EVALUATION CRITERIA				
	IMPACT ON THE CUSTOMER	RELATIONSHIP TO BUSINESS OBJECTIVES	NEED FOR IMPROVEMENT	RESOURCES REQUIRED	TOTAL
1. Equipment not properly installed					
2. Operators not trained					
3. Not enough time to comply with operating standards					
4. Work space too cluttered					

LEGEND: 3 = HIGH   2 = MEDIUM   1 = LOW

Figure 3-34

4.   Select one of the methods that follow for evaluating the options against the criteria.

    a. Numerical Rating

The numerical rating method uses a rating like 3 = High, 2 = Medium, and 1 = Low to define the relationship between each option and the criteria. (See Figure 3-33 for an example.)

    b. Point Scoring

        i. When the criteria selected are not equally important, each criterion can be weighted by assigning points. The points provide a maximum potential value for each criterion. The sum total of points assigned to all criteria must equal 100.

        ii. Each option is evaluated against the criteria and points are allocated up to the maximum allowed value assigned to that criterion. The total of all the points allocated during the evaluation does not have to equal, but can never exceed, 100.

        iii. Evaluate each option against all of the criteria before evaluating the next option.

An example of point scoring is shown in Figure 3-35.

PROBLEM-SELECTION MATRIX

PROBLEMS UNDER CONSIDERATION	EVALUATION CRITERIA				
	IMPACT ON THE CUSTOMER (50)	RELATIONSHIP TO BUSINESS OBJECTIVES (10)	NEED FOR IMPROVEMENT (30)	RESOURCES REQUIRED (10)	TOTAL MAX. (100)
1. Equipment not properly installed	10	10	25	10	55
2. Operators not trained	45	10	20	5	80
3. Not enough time to comply with operating standards	30	5	15	10	60
4. Work space too cluttered	10	3	30	3	46

(OPTIONS)

Figure 3-35

MATRIX

    c. *Scale*

       i. Another method for assigning a weight to the criteria when they are not equally important involves using a scale. To use this method, simply assign a value (1-5) to each criterion, but make certain that all high values are good and all low values are bad.

      ii. Evaluate all of the options against one criterion at a time.

An example of the use of a scale is shown in Figure 3-36.

PROBLEM-SELECTION MATRIX

PROBLEMS UNDER CONSIDERATION	EVALUATION CRITERIA				TOTAL
	IMPACT ON THE CUSTOMER 1 — 5 LOW HIGH	RELATIONSHIP TO BUSINESS OBJECTIVES 1 — 5 LOW HIGH	NEED FOR IMPROVEMENT 1 — 5 LOW HIGH	RESOURCES REQUIRED 1 — 5 HIGH LOW	
1. Equipment not properly installed	2	3	5	2	12
2. Operators not trained	4	3	4	4	15
3. Not enough time to comply with operating standards	1	5	3	2	11
4. Work space too cluttered	1	1	5	5	12

(OPTIONS)

Figure 3-36

5.   Define the relationship between the options and criteria by using one of the three methods just described. As a measure of the relationship between each option and criterion, a value is entered into the appropriate box on the matrix.

6. Total the values in each column and select the option with the highest score.

Helpful hints

1. When two or more of the options end up with similarly high scores, additional evaluation is necessary. In such cases, evaluate the options against additional criteria. Also, other tools for quality improvement, like the *INTERVIEW* and *SURVEY*, can be used to gather more information that can assist in making the selection.

2. Use *BRAINSTORMING* to identify a list of criteria that can be used in the matrix. Select those that are the most appropriate by using *LIST REDUCTION*.

3. To avoid bias in the evaluation, ensure that the criteria selected apply to every option under consideration.

PARETO CHART

PARETO CHART

Definition
Pareto analysis is the study of related subjects to determine if one is more significant than the others.[*]

Use
The Pareto chart is used to identify the most important item in a group of items. A Pareto chart breaks down an item into its component parts and then arranges and displays those parts in order of importance. Pareto analysis is used to focus problem-solving activities, so that the area causing the most difficulty is addressed first.

Example
In Figure 3-37, a family has compiled all of their unbudgeted expenses for the first six months of the year. A Pareto chart is used to display these expenses and arrange them so that the most significant expense item becomes obvious.

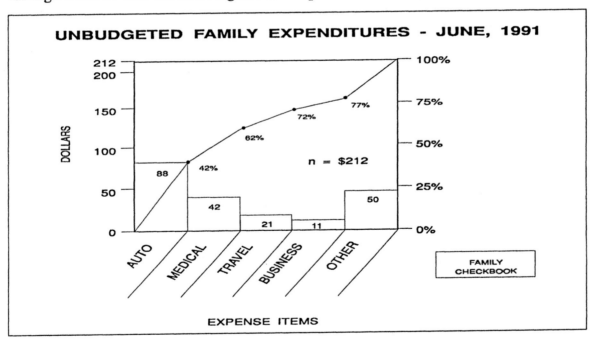

Figure 3-37

---

[*]   Vilfredo Pareto (1848–1923) studied the distribution of wealth in nineteenth- century Italy. He found that 80% of the wealth was controlled by 20% of the population. Upon examination, this 80/20 rule has since proved true in many other areas. The 80/20 split is often referred to as the "Pareto distribution." We use the Pareto distribution to achieve an 80% improvement by working on 20% of the causes. The Pareto chart was developed by Dr. Joseph Juran, an American quality control expert, who named it in honor of V. Pareto.

PARETO CHART

Step-by-step Instructions

1. Begin construction of the Pareto chart by accumulating the data to be analyzed.

2. Draw a rectangle. The vertical line on the left side of the rectangle (y-axis) is scaled to show the total amount of the item being analyzed. In Figure 3-37 this is the total amount of unbudgeted expenditures ($212). Place the total amount of the item under analysis at the upper left-hand corner of the rectangle and 0 at the lower left-hand corner. Next, scale the y-axis by placing hatch marks at intervals that fit the total number. (See also Figure 3-38.)

3. Divide the line at the bottom of the rectangle (x-axis) into equal spaces to represent the components of the item being analyzed. Write the name of each component underneath the x-axis. The components must be arranged according to size, largest to smallest, starting at the left. In Figure 3-38, the components are auto repair costs, medical expenses, etc.

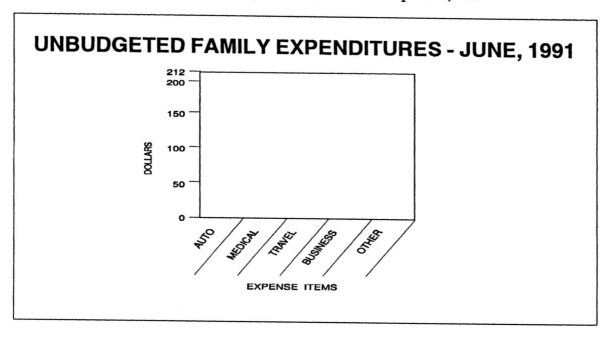

Figure 3-38

Occasionally, there will be several components with significantly less volume than the other components. In order not to complicate the Pareto chart, these items are totaled to create a component entitled "other." The "other" bar is always the last bar on the right, even if the sum of its components makes it taller than the other bars.

PARETO CHART

4.   Draw a bar for each component to a height that matches its frequency or count on the y-axis. In Figure 3-39 the auto expenditures bar has been constructed to a height of $88 on the y-axis; the medical expense bar to $42. The same has been done for all other bars/components. Note that the bars are constructed to touch one another. Also, if an "other" bar is used, construct it to a level equal to the sum of its components.

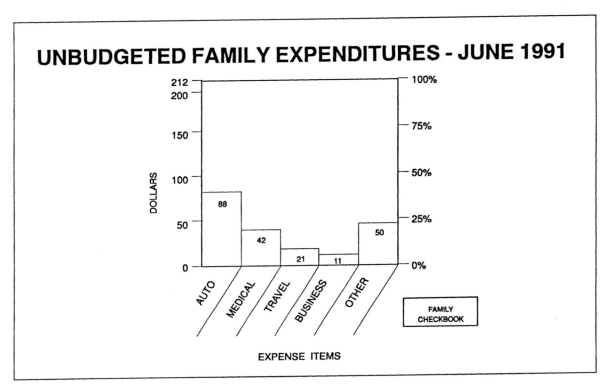

Figure 3-39

5.   The right-hand side of the pareto chart is scaled to show frequency by *percentage*. The top right-hand corner represents 100% and the bottom right-hand corner 0%. The percentage line should have hatch marks at 25%, 50%, and 75%.

6.   Calculate the percentage of the total represented by each component. For example, to determine the percentage that auto repair costs are of total unplanned expenditures, divide $88 by $212 and multiply by 100: 88 ÷ 212 × 100 = 41.5. This means that auto repair costs are 41.5% of total unplanned expenditures. Percentages for all other components are calculated in the same manner.

7. Draw a cumulative percentage line. To accomplish this, start at the lower left-hand corner of the rectangle and draw a line to the upper right-hand corner of the first bar. Place a dot at this point. In Figure 3-40 the dot falls on the top right-hand corner of the first bar. Next to the dot write the percentage calculated for the bar component. In our example, 41.5% has been rounded off to 42%.

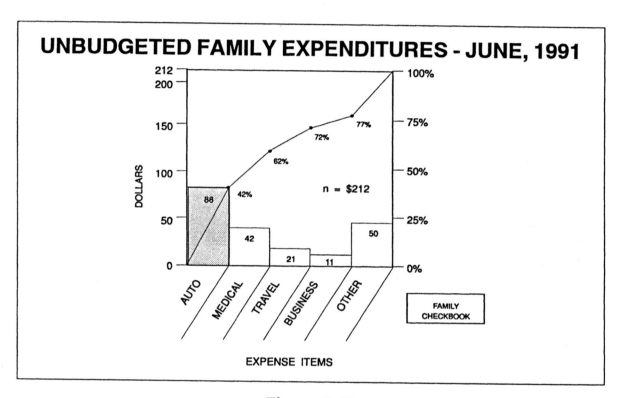

Figure 3-40

Next, identify the location of the second dot by adding the percentage of the second bar category to the first. In our example, medical expenses are 20% of total unplanned expenses (42 ÷ 212 = 19.8, rounded to 20). The second dot is on an imaginary line extending from $130 ($88 + $42) to 62% (20% + 42%) on the percentage line. It is also directly above the top right-hand corner of the second bar. The cumulative percentage amount (62%) is written next to the second dot.

Finish constructing the cumulative percentage line in the same manner, calculating the percentage of each component and accumulating the percentage total. Place dots above the top right-hand corner of the bar for each component and write the cumulative percentage amount next to the

PARETO CHART

dot. Finally, extend a line from the upper right-hand corner of the first bar to each of the dots in ascending order, ending at 100%.

8.   Write the total (n) of the components being analyzed in a clear space between the cumulative percentage line and the bars. Label the chart, including the date it was drawn, and provide a box that identifies the source of the data used.

Helpful hints

1.   Use Pareto analysis to reveal something of significance from information that otherwise remains unanalyzed and seemingly insignificant. For example, let's assume that you are wondering why your family budget is unbalanced after the first six months of the year. You look at your records and discover that there are 13 unplanned expenditures totaling $212. This information, by itself, is interesting but not of much use. Pareto analysis arranges the components of this amount so that you can determine the most significant expense, and take action based on what you discover.

2.   When the percentage of the component with the highest frequency or count is the largest percentage by far, and substantially more than the next largest component, it is most likely significant. Pareto analysis leads us to focus on the unexpected large category to find out why it has occurred. For example, our Pareto chart indicates that we had $88 in auto repair costs and only $42 in medical expenditures. The auto repair costs are significant enough to warrant our attention before addressing medical expenses. We may still want to address medical expenses, but not until actions have been taken to deal with the most significant source of our problem.

3.   To be of significance, the first component (bar) does not necessarily have to contain 80% of the total under analysis. The first bar should, however, be twice as large as the next biggest bar.

4.   A flat or somewhat level Pareto chart usually means that you need to examine the data further. Try looking at them from a different perspective. See if they can be broken down another way. Pareto analysis requires that you be creative. Break down the data in as many ways as possible in order to identify the most significant component.

PARETO CHART

5.   Use a "second-level" Pareto chart, to further analyze the major item in the first-level Pareto chart. This helps to pinpoint your analysis and aids in the search for root causes of the problem. In Figure 3-37, this means identifying the components of the auto repair costs.

6.   When you analyze, or break down an item by identifying its various components, maintain a consistent point of view. For instance, it would be a mistake to include planned expenditures with unplanned expenditures in the example we have been using.

PIE CHART

Definition
A pie chart illustrates the relative sizes of components that make up a whole.

Use
The pie chart is used to show how individual parts relate to the whole and to each other. Pie charts are often used to show when the size of a component has changed as a result of some action.

Example
In Figure 3-41 a pie chart is used to display the various sources of revenue for XYZ Manufacturing.

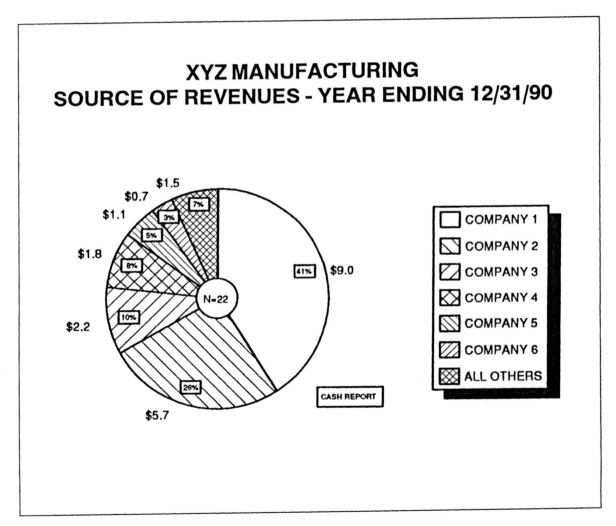

Figure 3-41

PIE CHART

Step-by-step Instructions

1. Identify the components of the pie chart and add up the quantities associated with them. To construct Figure 3-41 the following information was collected.

XYZ Manufacturing
Sources of 1990 Revenue (in $millions)

Company 1	$9.0
Company 2	5.7
Company 3	2.2
Company 4	1.8
Company 5	1.1
Company 6	.7
All Others	1.5
Total	$22.0

2. Calculate the percentage of the total attributable to each component. To accomplish this, divide each component by the total and multiply the result by 100. For example, Company 1 accounts for $9 million of XYZ's revenue and $22 million is the total revenue XYZ collected. Therefore the percentage of the total revenue received from Company 1 was $9 \div 22 \times 100 = 40.9\%$, rounded to 41%. Calculating the percentage of the total attributable to the other components is accomplished in the same manner.

3. Draw a wedge in the circle to represent the largest component. The components in the pie chart are arranged starting with the largest component and progressing to the smallest. The first line of the wedge representing the largest component is constructed by extending a line from the center of the circle straight up to the edge. This point on the edge of the circle represents the starting point for each component in the chart (0%) and the sum of all the components in the chart (100%).

4. Construct the second line of the wedge for the largest component by drawing a line from the center of the circle to a point that is representative of the percentage amount for this component. In Figure 3-41 the percentage amount attributable to the largest component is 41%. To find a point on the circle that is representative of 41%, visualize the pie chart as if it contained four equal segments, each 25% of the total. If each segment is

PIE CHART

25% of the total, segments 1 and 2 combine to equal 50% of the total, and segments 1, 2, and 3 equal 75% of the total. See Figure 3-42. Returning to our example, a point representative of 41% falls between 25% and 50%, and a little closer to 50%.

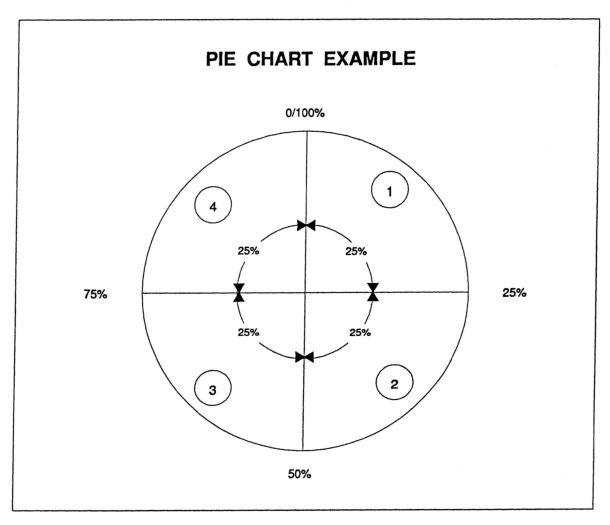

Figure 3-42

5.   Draw lines to represent the other components. Do this in the same fashion as before. Begin by adding the percentage for the second largest component to the first. In our example, Company 2 represents 26% of the total: 26% + 41% (Company 1) = 67%. A line representing this is drawn from the center of the circle to a point between 50% and 75%, and closer to 75%. Lines for the other components are drawn in the same manner.

6.   If the last components are too small to be easily read, group them together in an "other" category.

7.   Shade or draw hatch marks to distinguish one pie segment from another. Label each segment with numbers representing percentage of the total and volume of the component. In our example, the largest component is 41% of the total and $9 million in volume.

8.   Label the pie chart, provide source data, the number of components represented in the chart (12 in our example), and a legend to explain the shading or hatch mark scheme.

Helpful hints

1.   When two pie charts are used to communicate a change in the volume of one component, highlight only that component on both charts. Pie charts can be arranged in many ways to emphasize different points. Components can be "exploded" or slightly removed from the rest of the pie. Coloring or shading can be used to group segments. Some pie charts stress percentages, others stress the numbers.

2.   A pie chart conveys two pictures: an overall picture and a picture of the components that make up the whole. By comparison, a bar chart only shows how the individual components relate to one another; it doesn't communicate anything about the whole.

SURVEY

SURVEY

Definition
The survey is a means of gathering information using questionnaires.

Use
The survey is frequently used to understand and measure customer needs, attitudes, and satisfaction with products and services. It is best applied when the number of people to be questioned is large or difficult to speak with personally.

Example
The example of Figure 3-43 is a simple survey prepared by the Rachel's Restaurant to measure customer attitudes and satisfaction.

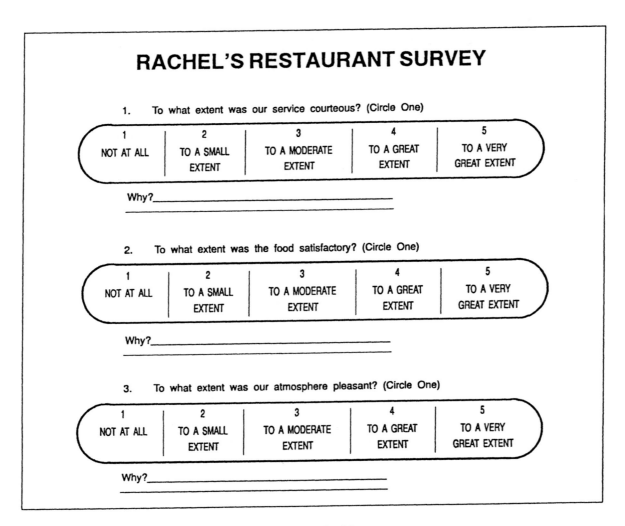

Figure 3-43

SURVEY

Step-by-step instructions

1. Verify that a survey is the best way to collect the information required. Sometimes, the information needed is already available. Also, consider other tools for quality improvement, like the *INTERVIEW*, that may be more appropriate for your situation.

2. Set objectives for the survey. Write objectives that clarify what you want to learn from the survey. One objective for the Rachel's Restaurant survey was to *"determine the extent to which customers enjoy the food we prepare."*

3. Identify who will be involved with the survey:

    - *How many surveys?:* Administered properly, surveys are proven (within bounds) to accurately judge the characteristics of a whole based on information obtained from part of the whole. The level of accuracy desired, or how certain you want to be of the survey findings, determines the number of surveys to be administered. To be reasonably certain about survey findings, at least 50 surveys must be completed.

    - *Who to survey?:* Survey different kinds of people to maintain the reliability of the survey, and include only people who are representative of the group about whom inferences will be made. For example, if Rachel's Restaurant wants to be certain about customer satisfaction, it should identify and prepare to survey each class of customer (age, sex, income, etc.) likely to buy its product. Placing a survey on the table, or on the back of a bill, satisfies this requirement.

4. Develop a set of questions to obtain the information required. Use questions that will achieve the objectives of the interview. Usually, the information gathered during a survey can be analyzed more easily if the questions require a numerical or objective response. Figure 3-44 associates potential answers with a scale to obtain responses that can be easily measured. True/False and Yes/No questions are also easy to evaluate.

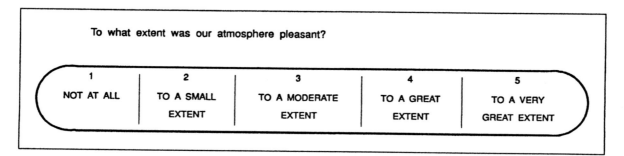

Figure 3-44

SURVEY

Include a few open-ended questions in the survey. These questions give the person responding an opportunity to add more than just a numerical or true/false response. Open-ended questions also are helpful for clarifying responses to objective questions. Examples of open-ended questions include: Why? How do you feel about...? What is your opinion? Why do you think this occurs? What would you do differently?

6. Determine what information you will want from those who complete the survey. Information about the survey respondents is useful for analyzing the survey data once they have been collected. Commonly obtained information includes

Position	Years of Service
Age	Income
Department	Experience

7. Organize the instructions and questions so that the survey will be easy to complete. Keep it simple. Provide instructions that include:

- why the survey is being conducted,
- how to fill out the survey, and
- where to return it.

8. Administer the survey to several people before sending it to the target group. Find out if it is easy to complete and if the responses provide the kind of information you want. Afterwards, make corrections as required.

9. When the surveys are returned, analyze them by looking for trends based on measurable evidence. The survey design will help make this task easy. Use other tools for quality improvement to organize and display the data, like a *CHECKSHEET, PARETO, BAR* or *PIE CHARTS*.

Helpful hints

1. If you have never conducted a survey before, it is a good idea to involve someone who has. Ask such a person to review the survey design. They should be able to offer some useful suggestions.

2. Surveys are a useful way of collecting information, but there is usually nothing to motivate someone to complete them. For this reason, it is

important to make certain the survey is easy to complete, not too long or confusing, and easy to return.

3.   One of the biggest problems with surveys is getting them back. Several methods can be utilized to encourage the survey recipients to complete and return surveys promptly:

- Have a recognized and respected person make the request in writing
- Provide a means for returning the completed survey that will not cost the respondent anything
- Offer an incentive for returning the completed survey (a pen, pin, opportunity to review the survey findings, etc.)
- Determine what you can about the climate surrounding those to be surveyed. Have they provided this information before? What is their general state of receptiveness toward the subject matter in the survey? Have they been asked to respond to other surveys recently?

Even when steps are taken to ensure that surveys will be returned, if a specific number of responses is required, send out more than that number to ensure that enough are returned to satisfy the requirement.

4.   Most survey forms are returned over a period of time. To compensate for this, ask for the survey to be returned by a date well in advance of the date you must have the survey information. This will allow time for surveys to be sent in late and provide time for a follow-up communication (if one is necessary) to those who have not returned their surveys on time.

Four

Applying the Tools for Quality Improvement

In previous chapters you have learned: (1) how the tools for quality improvement can help you think differently about what you do, (2) how the tools can be used with a set of problem-solving steps to reduce or eliminate process problems, and (3) how to apply the tools effectively. This chapter contains five case studies to summarize what you have read and help you visualize how the tools can be applied to solve actual work problems. Each case study describes a situation in which employees worked together to solve problems. The net effect of this teamwork is improved employee skills, better products, a better workplace, and improved customer satisfaction.

Following the case studies you will be introduced to the QI Story. The QI Story is a pictorial description of how the tools for quality improvement and problem-solving steps were used to solve a problem. The QI Story is a natural way to close this book, because its purpose is to summarize your problem-solving work and communicate to others what has been accomplished.

WHAT TO LOOK FOR IN THE CASES

There are some key elements that you should be aware of and look for in each case study. First, observe how the workers think about their problems as they apply the *new way of thinking* referred to in Chapter 1. These workers are not threatened by the problems they face, because of the confidence they have that the problems can be overcome. The employees you will read about use the tools for quality improvement with the skill of a brain surgeon or a master auto mechanic. They are familiar with the tools, feel secure in using them, and are motivated by the opportunity to apply them successfully to make needed improvements.

A second element to look for in the case studies is how effectively the tools can be applied with the *problem-solving steps*, even though the problems in each case study are different. By reading the case studies, it should become clear that the "new way of thinking" is embedded in the five problem-solving steps. As the workers in the case studies apply the steps, and complete the actions associated with them, they are actually thinking about their problems in a manner that is different from the way they thought about them before. They now recognize that problems can be solved and are committed to the improvement that can be achieved.

Finally, as you read the case studies, notice the *logic* in each application of the problem-solving steps and tools for quality improvement. The solutions make the problems appear easy to resolve, even when they were difficult, serious, and costly situations in need of improvement. In each case, a team of employees solved the problem convincingly. The recommended solutions were easy for management to approve, because they are based on facts that were communicated clearly with results to prove effectiveness.

CASE 1: MEASURING TRAINING EFFECTIVENESS

The Training Department of a large corporation was faced with a dilemma. It began when Bill Johnson, the Training Department Manager, was asked by his boss, "How do you know if your training programs are effective?"

The day after being confronted with this question, Bill called a meeting with his staff supervisors. Bill felt his department was providing effective training, but realized that he didn't have any facts on which to base his belief. He told his supervisors that he had been asked to develop and implement a means of evaluating training effectiveness. After much discussion, Bill and his staff supervisors decided to form a team. The team would be responsible for *developing a systematic approach to measure training effectiveness.* The team was to include members of the department who had been taught how to use the five problem-solving steps and tools for quality improvement.

Meeting 1

At their first meeting, Bill came in and described why the team had been formed. He told them he needed their involvement because of their knowledge and experience. The team also learned that Dale Peterson, one of Bill's supervisors, would act as team leader. Afterward, the team decided to call themselves "The Evaluators."

The Evaluators officially began the meeting by turning to the first problem-solving step, *Identify The Problem,* and reviewed the four actions necessary to complete this step:

   a. Identify something that needs improvement

   b. Show the need for improvement in measurable terms

   c. State the problem

   d. Establish an interim target and a date for achieving this improvement

The team felt that the first action was given them, but they struggled with the second action—*Show the need for improvement in measurable terms.* After a time, they realized that they were not dealing with a situation that could be resolved using the problem-solving process. Their task, they recognized, was to see if a problem existed, not to solve a problem. Without a systematic approach for measuring training effectiveness, there was no way to know if improvement was necessary. The team felt that the problem-solving steps would provide a

CASE 1: Measuring Training Effectiveness

logical thought process, though. So they developed the following statement to guide their actions: *"Training effectiveness is not being measured."*

Next, the team agreed to develop and implement a means of measuring training effectiveness within twelve weeks. Having established this interim target, the team shifted to the second-problem solving step, *Analyze.* They asked themselves, "How can we measure training effectiveness?" They decided to *BRAINSTORM* a list of ideas. Using the one-at-a-time approach, because they had a lot of ideas, the list in Figure 4-1 was developed.

WHAT CONSTITUTES EFFECTIVE TRAINING?

- Skilled instructors
- Only eligible people attend the training
- Interesting topics and discussion
- Comfortable environment
- Convenient location
- Correct materials available
- Appropriate training methods used
- Relevant training programs
- Course length matches time required to learn
- Activities stimulate participation
- Participants can apply what has been taught

Figure 4-1

The team wanted to identify the most significant items from this list, so they used *LIST REDUCTION* and narrowed the list to the following three:

1.   Only eligible people attend the training

2.   Skilled instructors

3.   Participants can apply what has been taught

CASE 1: Measuring Training Effectiveness

As the team ended the first meeting, Dale, the team leader, gave himself and the team an assignment. He told the team that he would identify and *INTERVIEW* representatives of training departments in other organizations to determine how they are measuring training effectiveness. He also asked the team members to locate and read books, articles, and other published documents that discuss how to measure training effectiveness. Dale said the interviews and research would be useful for analyzing the three measurement areas selected by the team.

Meeting 2

Dale reviewed the last meeting when the team met again. Then, he told the team that the interviews he conducted had verified that the three measurement areas selected by the team were consistent with what other companies were doing. Several team members pointed out that books and articles they had read also supported these three measures. Finally, Dale told the team that he discussed the three measurement areas with Bill Johnson and that Bill supported using them. The team agreed that this analysis satisfied the second problem-solving step.

To complete the third problem-solving step, *Evaluate Alternatives,* Dale asked the team to *BRAINSTORM* indicators for the three measurement areas. The team had several ideas, and quickly agreed to use the *number of ineligible participants/each class* for the first item: *Only eligible people attend the training.* As the team discussed this indicator, they realized that the Training Department had no direct control over the selection of participants who attend training programs. The team agreed that the only way the Training Department could affect this critical area was to collect data from each class, using the indicator they had identified, and provide this information to those who are responsible.

Agreeing on an indicator for the second measurement area, *instructor skill,* was also not difficult. The team decided to include the following question in a *SURVEY* that was being administered after each class. A *Line Graph* would be the indicator used to track the measurements. The survey question the team drafted is shown in Figure 4-2.

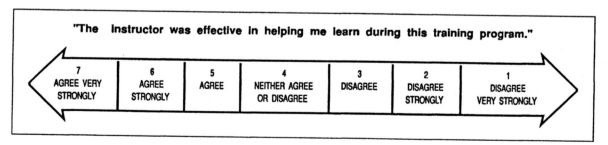

Figure 4-2

CASE 1: Measuring Training Effectiveness

An indicator for the third measurement area, *participants can apply what has been taught*, was more difficult for the team. The accepted idea came from team member Kim Reed. Kim described to the team how being able to *apply* what has been taught in a training program required that the participants *understand* what they were taught. Kim said she learned this from some research Dale asked the team to conduct after the first meeting. An article she read pointed out that "Pre/Post-Testing" is an effective way to measure the change in understanding that results from attending a training program. Pre/Post-testing, she told the team, involves testing each participant as he or she enters the class on the first day. Then, after the class is over, the same test is administered to the participants before they leave the class. Any change in test results can be directly attributed to the training experience. The team liked Kim's idea and agreed to use *HISTOGRAMS* to display the difference between Pre-test and Post-test results.

Next, the team prepared the *MATRIX* shown in Figure 4-3 to assemble and focus their thoughts.

HOW CAN TRAINING EFFECTIVENESS BE MEASURED?

ELEMENTS OF TRAINING EFFECTIVENESS	WHAT TO MEASURE	INDICATOR	WHEN TO MEASURE
ONLY ELIGIBLE PEOPLE ATTEND	RIGHT PEOPLE / RIGHT TRAINING PROGRAM	# OF INELIGIBLE PARTICIPANTS / ALL PARTICIPANTS	PRE-CLASS
SKILLED PROGRAM INSTRUCTORS	TEACHING EFFECTIVENESS	LINE GRAPH OF PARTICIPANT SURVEY RESPONSES	IN CLASS
PARTICIPANTS CAN APPLY WHAT HAS BEEN TAUGHT	AMOUNT OF LEARNING	% CHANGE IN PRE / POST-TEST RESULTS	IN CLASS

Figure 4-3

CASE 1: Measuring Training Effectiveness

Meeting 3

The team reviewed what they had accomplished in the first two meetings and then focused on planning the implementation of the three indicators they had identified. Again the team used *BRAINSTORMING* and *LIST REDUCTION* to develop the list of actions for each indicator shown in Figure 4-4.

	ACTIONS TO MEASURE TRAINING EFFECTIVENESS	
PRE-CLASS	RIGHT PEOPLE/ RIGHT TRAINING PROGRAM	- REVIEW COURSE ROSTERS TO IDENTIFY INELIGIBLE PARTICIPANTS - COMMUNICATE NUMBER OF INELIGIBLE PARTICIPANTS TO THOSE RESPONSIBLE - IMPLEMENT/MONITOR INDICATOR
IN CLASS	TEACHING EFFECTIVENESS	- INCLUDE INSTRUCTOR EVALUATION WITH END-OF-COURSE EVALUATIONS
IN CLASS	AMOUNT OF LEARNING	- DEVELOP/IMPLEMENT PRE/POST-TESTS FOR SELECTED COURSES

Figure 4-4

Next, the team used *BARRIERS & AIDS* to identify difficulties that might be encountered when their proposed actions were implemented. This tool also helped to identify additional actions (aids) to counter these barriers; they were added to the existing list of planned actions, as shown in Figure 4-5.

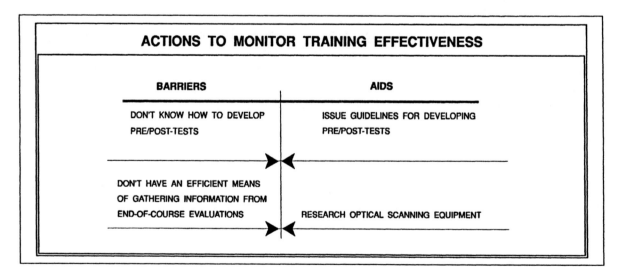

Figure 4-5

CASE 1: Measuring Training Effectiveness

With the implementation plan completed, the team was ready to move into the fourth problem-solving step, *TEST-IMPLEMENT*. Before doing this, they needed to meet with Bill Johnson to present their ideas and obtain his approval to proceed. The team agreed to invite Bill and his supervisors to their next meeting. Each team member was given an assignment to prepare part of the materials required for the presentation.

Meeting 4

The team's presentation went well. Bill and his supervisors were impressed with the team's accomplishments and approved their recommendations for implementation.

Meeting 5

Several team members volunteered to complete the various actions listed on the implementation plan. They also agreed to meet informally over the next couple weeks after the indicators were put in place and data began to be collected. The next formal meeting was scheduled for five weeks later.

Meeting 6

The team members shared findings from the indicators that had been implemented and were being monitored. The *LINE GRAPH* of ineligible participants is shown in Figure 4-6.

The *LINE GRAPH* of *SURVEY* responses monitoring instructor skills is shown in Figure 4-7.

HISTOGRAMS of Pre/Post test results are shown in Figure 4-8.

The team discussed the three indicators that had been implemented, and several ideas evolved.

- All of the team members agreed that the *LINE GRAPH* for ineligible participants appeared to be improving. But the team wondered if it would continue to improve, and what could be done to maintain this improvement.

- Looking at the *LINE GRAPH* of survey responses monitoring instructor skill, the team was concerned about the one low rating in class 5.

- The team was pleased with how clearly the *HISTOGRAMS* displayed the improvement in test results. The histograms helped prove that participants were prepared to apply what they had learned after attending the training program. The team did wonder, though, what could be done to improve the post-test results.

CASE 1:Measuring Training Effectiveness

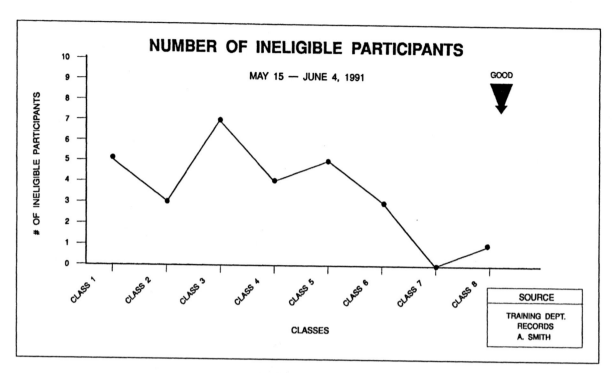

Figure 4-6

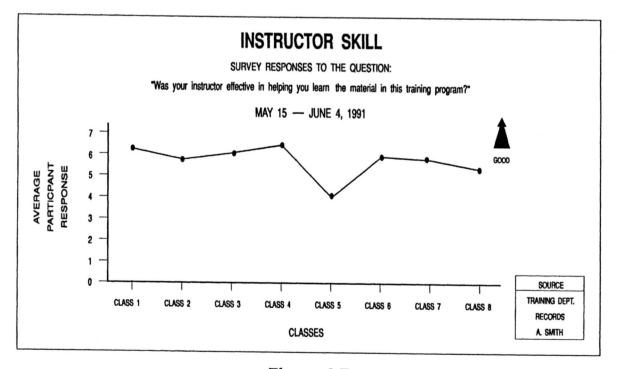

Figure 4-7

CASE 1: Measuring Training Effectiveness

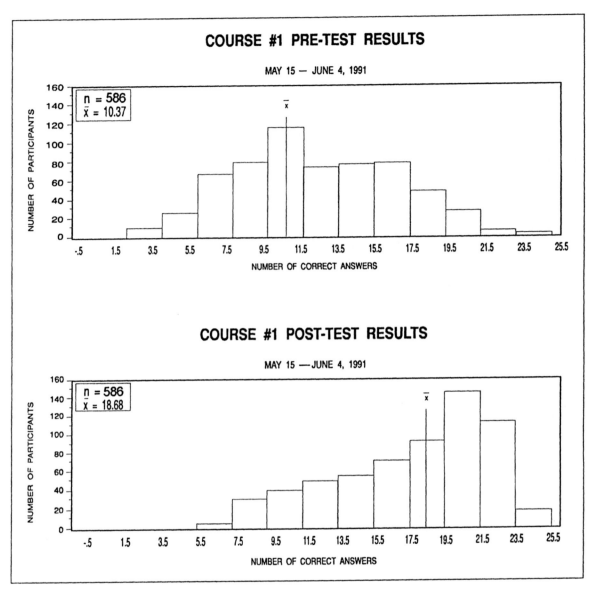

Figure 4-8

The team agreed to present these findings to Bill and his supervisors at their next meeting. The team wanted to hear Bill's reaction and decided to request permission to apply the problem-solving steps to improve post-test results. In addition, they would seek approval to complete the fifth problem-solving step, *Standardize,* by making the three indicators permanent measures of training effectiveness.

CASE 2: SUGGESTIONS ANYONE?

The suggestion program at Marquette Industries, a large commercial construction company, was not generating many ideas. Over the years some good ideas had been submitted, many contributing valuable cost savings, but the number of suggestions had dropped off steadily in recent years. Marquette's senior management wanted to turn this trend around. Marquette realized the value of its employees and their ability to suggest ways to improve Marquette's operations.

A team of employees was formed to investigate the declining participation in the suggestion program. The team was comprised of employees from several work locations. Prior to their first meeting, the team was assembled and given the task: *Increase employee participation in the suggestion program.* A team leader was assigned, and the team was told they would be reporting their findings and recommendations to Shawn O'Reilly, vice president of Construction Services.

Meeting 1

At their first meeting the team considered problem-solving step one, *Identify The Problem.* They agreed that a problem had been identified, but recognized they didn't have a way to show the need for improvement in measurable terms. To satisfy this requirement, the team researched available information to compare Marquette with other companies in their industry that had suggestion programs. They plotted the percent of employees participating in the suggestion program over the last five years on a *LINE GRAPH* to give a clear picture of how Marquette compared with the other companies. See Figure 4-9.

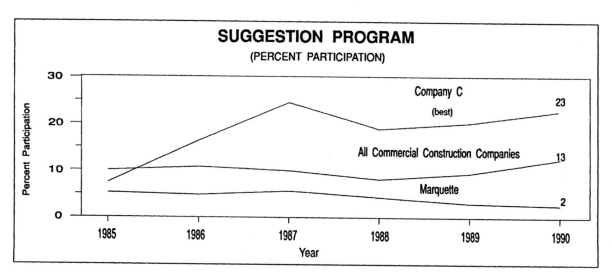

Figure 4-9

CASE 2: Suggestions Anyone?

Based on this information, the team agreed on the following problem statement: *Participation in Marquette's suggestion program is equivalent to only 9% of the rate for the best commercial construction company.* In fact, Marquette's participation rate was so low that it would have to be increased by 650% to equal the industry average. The team responded by setting an aggressive interim target for improvement: Increase Marquette's suggestion program participation rate to 15% by year end.

Meetings 2 - 4

In their next meeting the team began the second problem-solving step, *Analyze.* They decided to use *CAUSE-AND-EFFECT ANALYSIS* and began by *BRAINSTORMING* causes of the effect (problem): *"participation in Marquette's suggestion program is equivalent to only 9% of the rate for the best commercial construction company."* The team grouped together related potential causes from the brainstorm list, and the "major bones" were identified as

> A. Awards/Recognition
>
> B. Suggestion Evaluation/Implementation
>
> C. Program Awareness
>
> D. Suggestion Procedure

This done, the team began to construct the fishbone diagram. They used the items from the brainstorm list to add potential causes to the corresponding major bones. The team then went further into the analysis by asking, "What causes this to occur?" of each potential cause. The team went as deep as they could in the investigation of causes contributing to the problem. Next, they reviewed the diagram, checking to ensure that true cause-and-effect relationships existed from each bone back to the problem statement. Finally, items were highlighted that appeared to be root causes of the problem. See Figure 4-10.

Meetings 5 - 6

A *SURVEY* was planned to verify that the highlighted items in the *CAUSE-AND-EFFECT ANALYSIS* were root causes of the problem and not symptoms. The survey involved a broad range of Marquette's employees. Findings from the survey are shown in Figure 4-11.

CASE 2: Suggestions Anyone?

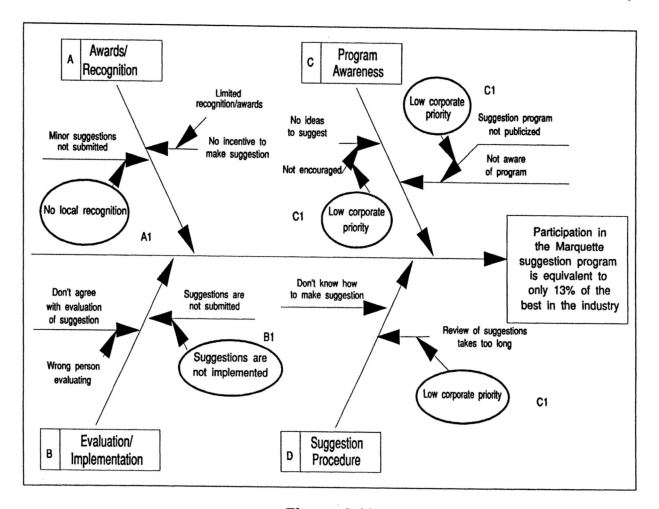

Figure 4-10

	ROOT CAUSE	SURVEY FINDINGS
A1	No local recognition	78% of the employees surveyed wanted recognition from local management
C1	Suggestions are not implemented	80% said seeing their ideas implemented was the prime motivator for submitting ideas
C1	Low corporate priority	37% did not know how to submit a suggestion
		42% said it takes too long to see results

Figure 4-11

CASE 2: Suggestions Anyone?

Meeting 7

The survey findings led the team to conclude that the first two root causes (A1 and B1) were primarily responsible for the problem. But they also agreed that the third root cause (C1) would be easy to resolve, so they planned to address that, too. The team then moved on to the third problem-solving step, *Evaluate Alternatives*.

Each root cause was written on a flip chart pad. *BRAINSTORMING* was used to generate alternative solutions that would solve or eliminate each root cause. Five potential solutions were identified and expanded by developing the activities required for implementation. Next, the potential effectiveness of each alternative was determined by comparing them against the following criteria:

- degree of impact on the customer,
- timeliness of implementation,
- ease of implementation, and
- need for improvement.

The team used a *MATRIX* (see Figure 4-12) to organize their thinking and to facilitate the process of evaluating the alternative solutions. The normal two-sided matrix was expanded slightly to clarify the relationship between the root causes and the activities needed to reduce or eliminate them. Numerical rating was the method chosen by the team to evaluate each solution activity against the criteria. The activities with the highest total score were selected (shaded) for implementation. The team was confident that, if implemented properly, these solutions would lead to their target of 15% participation by year end.

To close the meeting, assignments were made within the team to prepare a detailed implementation plan for each solution.

Meeting 8

The assignments were reviewed and a *BARRIERS & AIDS* analysis was conducted on the implementation plan for each solution to ensure that the plan was comprehensive. The team then agreed to present their recommendations to management. Additional assignments were made within the team to prepare for the presentation.

Meeting 9

Shawn O'Reilly, vice president of Construction Services, was excited by the team's presentation and gave them authorization to proceed with their implementation plans.

CASE 2: Suggestions Anyone?

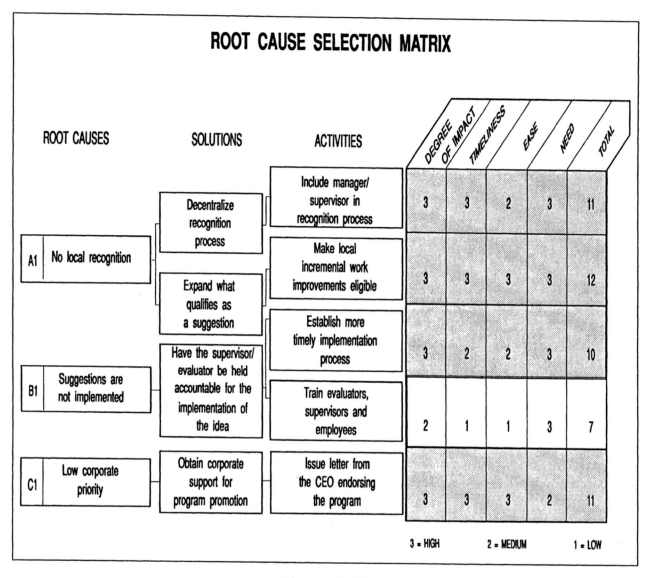

Figure 4-12

Meetings 10 - 13

The implementation plan to reduce or eliminate the root causes was carried out by the team members. When these assignments were completed, the team conducted periodic checks to ensure that everything was going as planned. Only minor adjustments to the implementation plan were necessary.

CASE 2: Suggestions Anyone?

Year End

The team's solutions and implementation plan had a remarkable effect. Percent participation in the suggestion program increased from 2% to 19.2%, as shown in the *LINE GRAPH* of Figure 4-13.

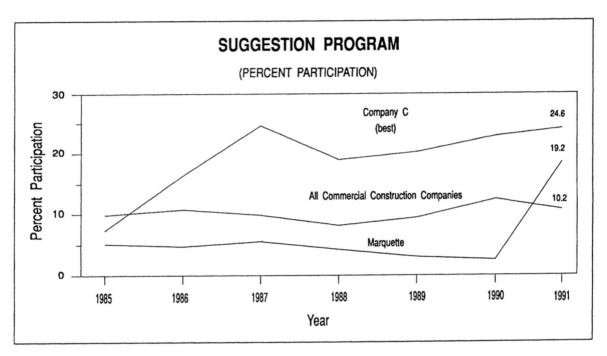

Figure 4-13

Meeting 14

The team met to complete the fifth problem-solving step, *Standardize*. Actions they planned to recommend to Mr. O'Reilly were:

- Include information about the suggestion program in training programs.

- Encourage suggestions that affect local work areas.

- Publish good suggestion examples to improve the quality of suggestions.

- Clearly assign and communicate responsibility for the number of suggestions implemented as a percentage of all suggestions submitted.

CASE 3: HANDLING CUSTOMER INQUIRIES

Lancet Industries, a large retail sales organization, decided that quality of service could be improved if teams were formed to work on problems common to several work areas. This idea was promoted by senior management, and volunteers for team membership were requested from several departments. The employees who volunteered were given a day and a half of intensive training in the use of the five problem-solving steps and the tools for quality improvement. Selected employees were then chosen to lead the teams and received an additional three days of training. Lancet's Customer Service Department formed one such team.

Meeting 1

The Customer Service team began by discussing their purpose and the rules of order under which they would operate. They decided when they would meet, discussed who would be responsible for the minutes for each meeting, learned who the team would report to (management sponsor), and reviewed the problem-solving steps.

Having taken care of these essential administrative activities, the team turned to the first problem-solving step, *Identify The Problem*. Because they did not have a problem assigned to them, the team *BRAINSTORMED* a list of improvement opportunities (common work problems). This list was not complete by the end of the meeting, so the team leader, Alice Cook, suggested to the team that before the next meeting they review the list that had been compiled, and ask for additional ideas from co-workers who were not part of the team.

Meeting 2

The second meeting began with a review of what happened during the first meeting. The team then quickly finished adding to the list of improvement opportunities. *LIST REDUCTION* was used to reduce the list to five improvement opportunities. Next, the team developed a *MATRIX* and used point scoring to select "timely response to customer correspondence" as the area where the team would focus their problem-solving skills. This was an area where many of the team members had heard complaints from customers who called to voice disappointment that their inquiries had not been answered.

To show the need for improvement in measurable terms, the team decided to track the number of written customer inquiries that were not answered when they should have been. The team was uncertain of a reasonable time limit for answering a customer inquiry, so Alice, the team leader, checked with the team's sponsor. He

CASE 3: Handling Customer Inquiries

confirmed that the period of time between receiving and answering a customer inquiry should be no more than five working days.

To close the meeting, several team members were assigned the task of reviewing all customer inquiries received since April 8. In this review the team members were to use a *CHECKSHEET* to record the number of customer inquiries not answered in five days.

Meeting 3

The *CHECKSHEET* developed by the team members revealed that 61 of 210 (29%) of all customer inquiries for the period reviewed had not been answered in five days. Based on this data, the team developed a *LINE GRAPH* to indicate the need for improvement in measurable terms. See Figure 4-14.

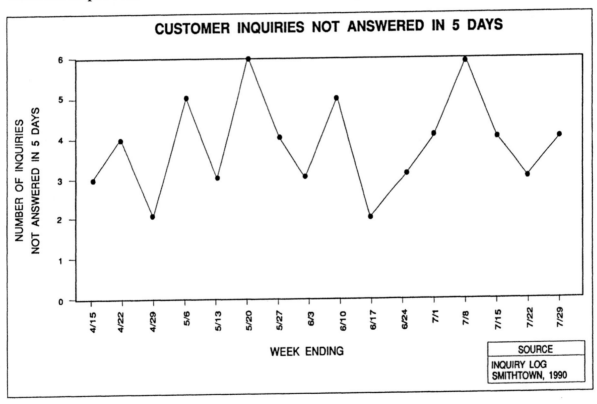

Figure 4-14

The team ended their third meeting by completing the first problem-solving step and agreeing on the problem statement: *Between April 15 and July 29, 1990, 29% of customer inquiries were not answered in five working days.* The team also agreed on an interim target and date for achieving it: *Achieve a 50% reduction in unanswered customer inquiries by December 31, 1990.*

CASE 3: Handling Customer Inquiries

Meeting 4

To address the second problem solving step, *Analyze,* the team developed a *FLOWCHART* of the activities involved in the current process for responding to customer inquiries. See Figure 4-15.

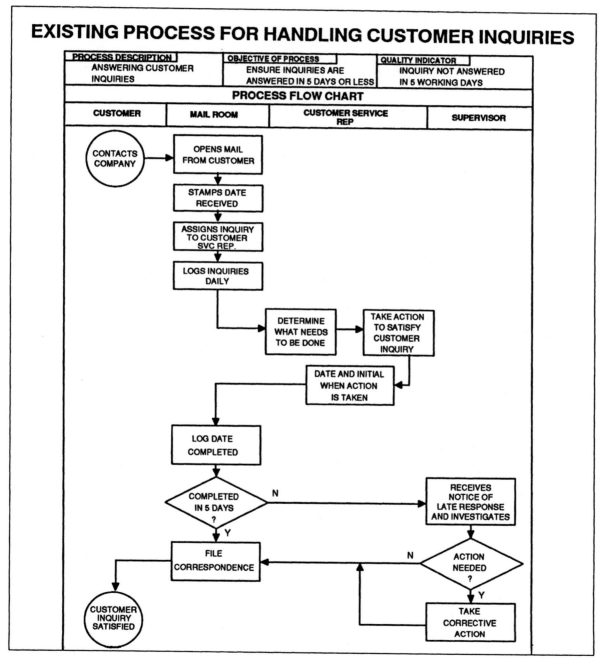

EXISTING PROCESS FOR HANDLING CUSTOMER INQUIRIES

PROCESS DESCRIPTION	OBJECTIVE OF PROCESS	QUALITY INDICATOR
ANSWERING CUSTOMER INQUIRIES	ENSURE INQUIRIES ARE ANSWERED IN 5 DAYS OR LESS	INQUIRY NOT ANSWERED IN 5 WORKING DAYS

PROCESS FLOW CHART

CUSTOMER	MAIL ROOM	CUSTOMER SERVICE REP	SUPERVISOR

Figure 4-15

CASE 3: Handling Customer Inquiries

Meeting 5

The existing process for answering customer inquiries looked like it should work effectively. So the team decided to investigate each time a customer inquiry was not responded to in five working days during the period April 15 to July 29, 1990. The *PARETO CHART* in Figure 4-16 was used to display the reasons for slow response time.

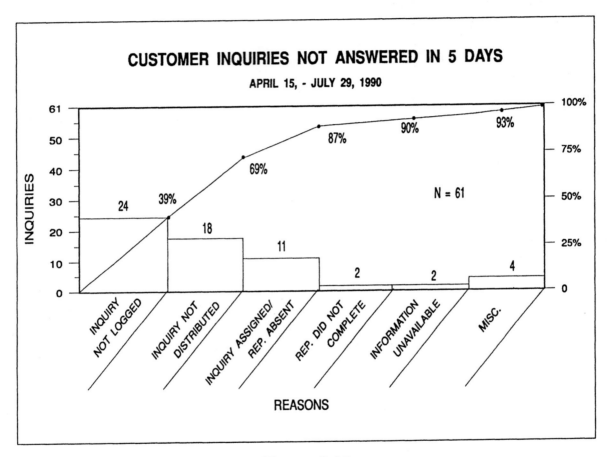

Figure 4-16

The Pareto analysis verified that 87% of the inquiries exceeding the five-day limit were caused by the following three factors:

1.   *Inquiry not logged:* All incoming mail received a date stamp on the day it was received, but 39% of the inquiries exceeding the five-day limit were not logged in as having been assigned to a customer service representative on the day they were received.

CASE 3: Handling Customer Inquiries

2.   *Inquiry not distributed:* 30% of the inquiries exceeding the five-day limit were logged in and assigned on the day they were received, but were not distributed to the customer service representative for several days.

3.   *Inquiry assigned/rep absent:* Inquiries assigned to representatives who were not available at the time work was assigned accounted for 18% of the inquiries exceeding the five-day limit.

The team decided to address each of these three root causes. The Pareto analysis made it clear that the employees in the mail room were unaware that their actions effected a timely response to customer inquiries. The team agreed that any solutions implemented must target the mail room, but should in no way make the mail room employees feel "guilty" for their actions.

Meeting 6

The team moved on to the third problem-solving step, *Evaluate Alternatives.* Solutions were *BRAINSTORMED* to correct the three root causes of the problem. A *MATRIX* was used to evaluate each solution against criteria that included: cost efficient, customer oriented, ease of implementation, and potential effectiveness. Three solutions were selected:

1.   Assign a person to the mail room to log and distribute customer inquiries each day between 8-9 A.M.

2.   Ensure that customer inquiries are assigned to customer service representatives daily.

3.   Distribute inquiries to available customer service representatives only.

The team performed a *BARRIERS & AIDS* analysis to identify problems that might be encountered with the implementation of their solutions. This analysis led the team to edit the first solution. It was revised to read: *Assign a customer service representative to the mail room to log and distribute customer inquiries each day between 8-9 A.M.* The team felt that this change in their solution:

   ■ clarified where the additional person in the mail room would come from,

   ■ assigned a person to the mail room who was familiar with what must be done, and

   ■ ensured that the assigned person knew who was available to work on inquiries.

CASE 3: Handling Customer Inquiries

The team ended the meeting by agreeing to invite their sponsor to the next meeting. Each team member shared in completing the various responsibilities necessary to present their findings.

Meeting 7

The sponsor thought the team's solutions were excellent, and agreed to *TEST-IMPLEMENT* them beginning the following week.

During the five-week test implementation, different team members worked in the mail room between 8–9 A.M. to log and distribute customer inquiries. While there, these team members learned how the solutions were working, and suggested a minor modification to the first solution. The modification addressed the fact that a customer service representative was only needed in the mail room for 5–10 minutes each morning; an hour wasn't necessary.

Meeting 8

The effect of the team's actions was added to the existing *LINE GRAPH; see* Figure 4-17.

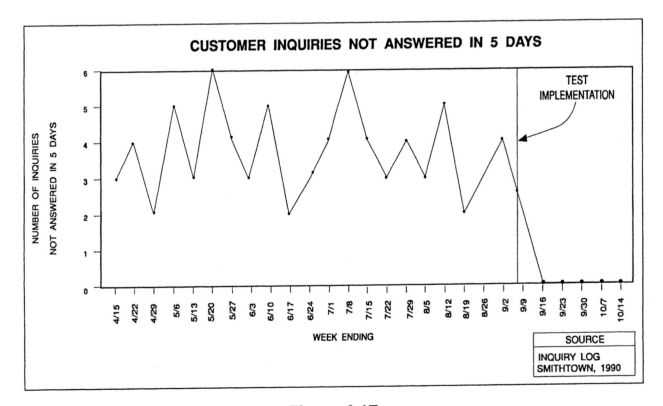

Figure 4-17

CASE 3: Handling Customer Inquiries

Their solutions working effectively, the team worked to complete the fifth problem-solving step, *Standardize*. They revised the *FLOWCHART* that had been developed in Step 2. This would help maintain the gains that had been achieved by ensuring that each employee involved in the process knew what he or she was supposed to do and why. The changes made to the process are highlighted in Figure 4-18.

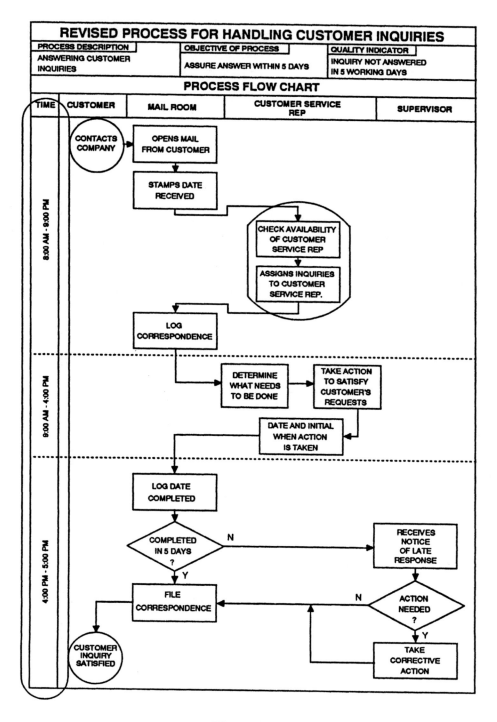

Figure 4-18

CASE 3: Handling Customer Inquiries

Finally, the team considered whether other departments might benefit from their efforts. No other applications were evident, so the team concluded the assignment by preparing a final presentation to the sponsor. This presentation was a huge success for all involved.

CASE 4: PROCESSING INVOICES FOR PAYMENT

Siscon Bolt and Screw was a profitable company with a reputation for not paying their bills on time. Things were so bad at Siscon that many of their suppliers had ceased doing business with them. At first, Siscon's management didn't mind when suppliers dropped them, because there were plenty of other suppliers who were happy to get Siscon's business. But management got involved when a big sale was missed because Siscon couldn't get the supplies they needed to meet a customer's deadline. When the incident was investigated, management found out that the supplier wouldn't ship the materials needed for the sale because three of their invoices remained unpaid.

The event caused management to form a team to investigate why it took so long to pay an invoice. The team that was formed reported directly to Ralph Tiotinotti, vice president of Sales. The team leader was production manager Terry Girr, and included people from various functional areas, including Production, Accounting, Finance, Engineering, and Sales. The objective of the team was to: *Improve the efficiency of invoice processing.*

Meeting 1

After the customary administrative matters were taken care of, the team quickly began applying the five problem-solving steps. The team members were all trained to use the tools for quality improvement and had applied the five-step process before.

To show the need for improvement in measurable terms, the team decided to measure the "number of invoices not paid on time." But first, they needed to develop an operational definition for "on time." The team members from Accounting and Finance helped with this, and their input was confirmed by upper management with the influence of Mr. Tiotinotti. "On time" was defined as *paying an invoice in time to take advantage of discounts offered, and before late charges are assessed. Invoices that do not offer discounts, or do not assess late charges, are considered paid "on time" when paid within 30 days of receipt.*

With the measure defined, the team decided to use two indicators. First, a *LINE GRAPH* would be used to provide an overall picture of the problem, and second, a *PIE CHART* would provide a monthly breakdown of the invoices not paid on time. To end the first meeting, Terry assigned several members the task of obtaining the data necessary to construct the two indicators.

Meetings 2 - 4

The team reviewed the minutes of the first meeting and then looked at the *LINE GRAPH* and *PIE CHART* that had been prepared since the last meeting.

CASE 4: Processing Invoices for Payment

Additional information from this research uncovered that Siscon received an average of 210 invoices each month, 78% of which were not paid on time according to the operational definition. This information was based on the five months studied, excluding December, when a concerted effort was put forth by the Accounting Department to pay as many outstanding invoices as possible in order to maximize tax write-offs for the fiscal year ended December 31, 1990. See Figure 4-19 for the *LINE GRAPH* and Figure 4-20 for the *PIE CHART.*

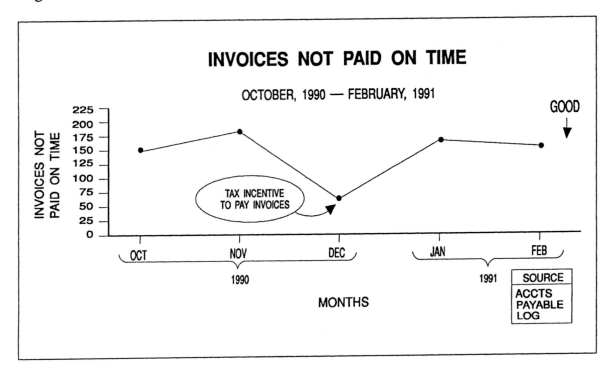

Figure 4-19

With this information in hand, the team developed the following problem statement: *Invoices not paid on time averaged 78% between October 1990 and February 1991.* In addition, the team set the following interim target: *Achieve a 30% reduction in the average number of invoices not paid on time by June 30, 1991.*

To address problem-solving step 2, *Analyze*, the team developed a *Flowchart* of the current invoice payment process (see Figure 4-21). After developing the flowchart, the team needed to know which activities in the process were taking the most time. To obtain this information, they identified a measure for each major step within the process.

CASE 4: Processing Invoices for Payment

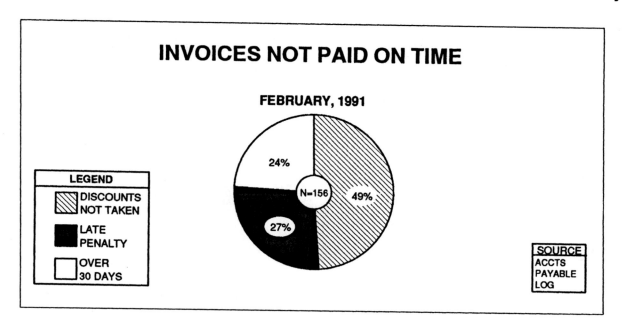

Figure 4-20

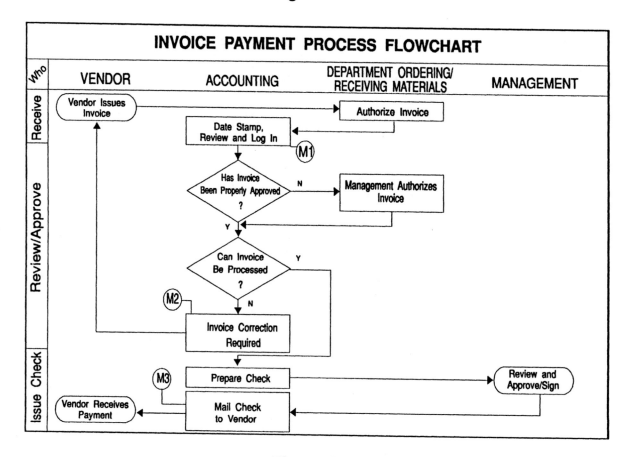

Figure 4-21

CASE 4: Processing Invoices for Payment

The team enhanced an existing log in the Accounting Department to track all three measures:

M1.   Number of days from the date the invoice was received at Siscon to the date received by Accounting.

M2.   Number of days invoices returned to vendor.

M3.   Number of days from invoice receipt in accounting to date mailed.

Meetings 5 - 7

The team developed a *CAUSE-AND-EFFECT DIAGRAM*. The major steps in the invoice payment process were used as the major "bones" on the diagram; see Figure 4-22.

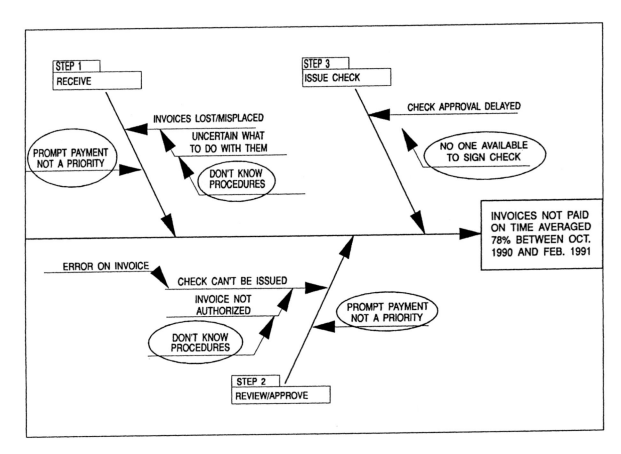

Figure 4-22

CASE 4: Processing Invoices for Payment

Three potential root causes (highlighted in Figure 4-22) were verified by *INTERVIEWS* with people in the Accounting Department and in other departments that received a large number of invoices. The team studied the log that was tracking the three process measures to decide which root cause to attack first. They discovered that delays were occurring at each major step in the process. Therefore, the team agreed to address all three root causes in the third problem-solving step, *Evaluate Alternatives*.

Meeting 8

Several alternative solutions were generated using *BRAINSTORMING*; see Figure 4-23.

SOLUTIONS
1. Communicate the operational definition of "on time," and inform everyone involved with invoice processing that Siscon wants to pay its bills "on time."
2. Develop a set of invoice processing procedures and communicate it to everyone involved, including vendors.
3. Provide a select number of managers with check signing authority to ensure that someone is available to sign checks.

Figure 4-23

BARRIERS & AIDS analysis was used to identify potential problems with the implementation of these solutions. Several good ideas came up and were included in an implementation plan. The team agreed to present their findings to Mr. Tiotinotti at their next meeting.

Meetings 9 - 11

Mr. Tiotinotti was impressed with the team's findings and was amazed that the improvements would not be costly to implement. He agreed to let the team test-implement their solutions in order to assess how effectively they reduced the problem. After each solution was implemented, the team continued to track the time required to handle each invoice during the three major process steps. The overall effect of the team's actions is shown in the *LINE GRAPH* of Figure 4-24.

A *PIE CHART* for the invoices paid during May was also prepared; see Figure 4-25.

CASE 4: Processing Invoices for Payment

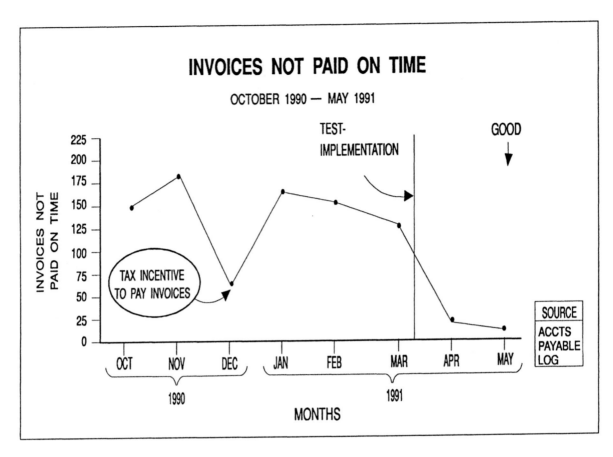

Figure 4-24

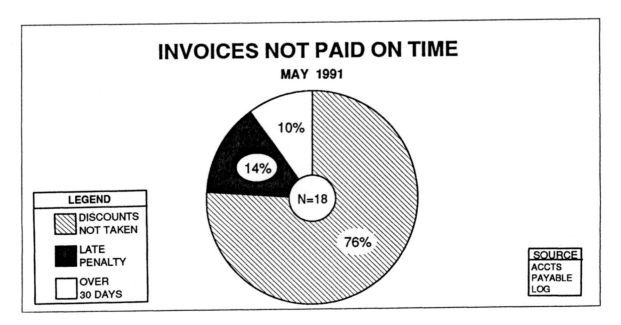

Figure 4-25

CASE 4: Processing Invoices for Payment

Meeting 12

The team's final solution included something they learned during the test-implementation. They had discovered that by adding an activity to the invoice payment process—*Review invoices for discounts and late penalties*—more invoices were being paid on time. The team worked with Accounting to implement this change to the process and prepared another *FLOWCHART* to ensure that everyone understood how the process was supposed to work.

To complete the fifth problem-solving step, *Standardize,* the team obtained approval from Mr. Tiotinotti to make the solutions permanent. They also recommended that the problem-solving steps be applied to determine why "Discounts not taken" accounted for 76% of the invoices not paid on time in May.

CASE 5: IMPROVING EMPLOYEE SAFETY

Larry's Lumber had just completed a lengthy contract negotiation with the IBLW (International Brotherhood of Lumber Workers). The IBLW represented approximately 70% of Larry's work force. At times during the contract negotiations, the issue of safety was a hot topic, as union representatives wanted management to be more committed to worker safety. But when the contract was finally approved, other issues on the bargaining table took precedence, and safety was not addressed.

Employee safety was not forgotten by Larry Steadman, the owner of Larry's Lumber. He wanted the employees to know that safety was more than just a word tossed around the bargaining table. His concern for safety was real, and he decided to take action. He formed a team, and assigned them responsibility for: *Reducing the company's accident rate.*

Heading up the team was "Big" Al Arnold, a former union representative now working as a line manager. Al was a tough, but fair man, who was two years from retirement. He looked at this assignment as an opportunity to do something positive for a company where he had worked his entire adult life. He told Larry that he would take on this challenge, but first it had to be narrowed down.

"What do you mean?" Larry asked.

Al told him that there are many kinds of accidents. Minor incidents, like a bruise or small laceration, and major accidents, like the time one of the workers almost lost an arm trying to service a piece of equipment. The worker's arm was saved, but Al never forgot the incident.

Larry understood Al's concern. The problem was not specific enough to tackle in its present form. They agreed that Al and his team would focus on accidents requiring a visit to a doctor, a "doctor case" as they were referred to within the company.

Meeting 1

Most of the first meeting was spent taking care of administrative issues, but before the meeting ended, Al and the team did get started applying the first problem-solving step, *Identify The Problem.* The problem had already been identified, so the team began to discuss ways of showing the need for improvement in measurable terms. One of the team members, Becky Poindexter, pointed out that records of doctor cases were maintained in the Safety Department. Since Becky worked in that department, she volunteered to use this data to create a *LINE GRAPH.*

CASE 5: Improving Employee Safety

Between meetings, as Becky began constructing the line graph, she recognized that this indicator could serve dual purposes. First, it would show the number of doctor cases that occurred each month, and, second, the graph would display a twelve-month running total of these accidents. This would help track performance trends.

Meeting 2

After Al quickly reviewed the minutes of the first meeting, Becky gave each member of the team a copy of the line graph she had prepared; see Figure 4-26.

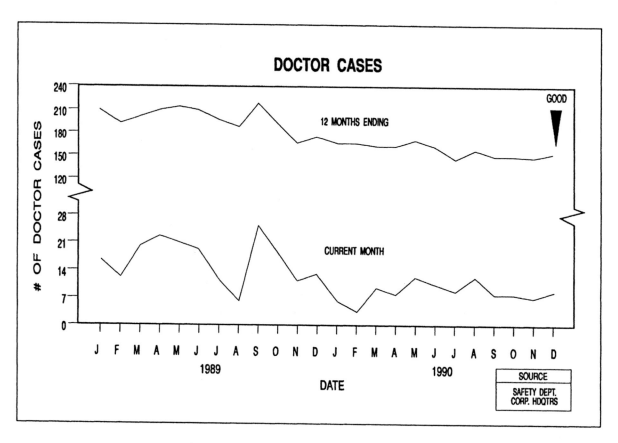

Figure 4-26

The team agreed that the line graph showed the extent of the problem well, but did not feel comfortable developing a problem statement from what they saw.

CASE 5: Improving Employee Safety

They decided to construct a *BAR CHART* of doctor cases by department to see if a problem became more apparent; see Figure 4-27.

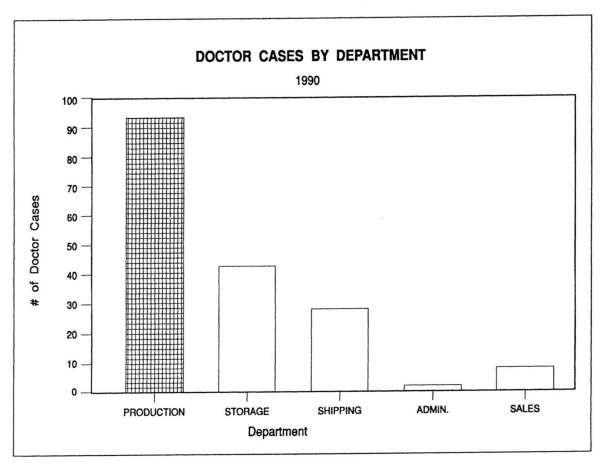

Figure 4-27

This breakdown of information was helpful to the team. They agreed to narrow their investigation to the Production Department, because it was the largest single contributor to doctor cases at Larry's Lumber. The team also was certain that what they learned from an investigation of doctor cases in the Production Department could be applied to reduce their occurrence in other departments. Becky had brought data to the team meeting related to the Production Department's doctor cases, so the team spent the balance of the meeting studying the 93 doctor cases that had occurred during 1990. They stratified these doctor cases by "types of injury" using a *PARETO CHART*; see Figure 4-28.

CASE 5: Improving Employee Safety

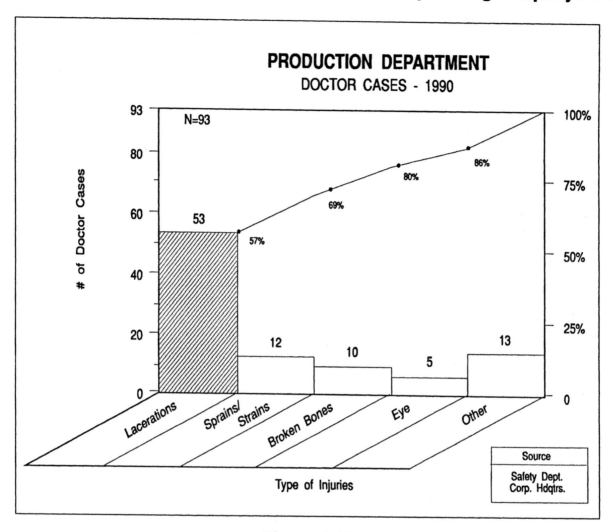

PRODUCTION DEPARTMENT

DOCTOR CASES - 1990

Figure 4-28

As the meeting closed, Al and the team agreed that it would be helpful to further analyze the data on lacerations—to show the "body part injured." Two team members volunteered to complete a Pareto chart showing this breakdown before the next meeting.

CASE 5: Improving Employee Safety

Meetings 3 - 5

The second-level Pareto chart (Figure 4-29) clearly identified a problem the team could address. They developed the following problem statement: *"40% of the doctor cases in the Production Department involved lacerations to the hand or fingers."*

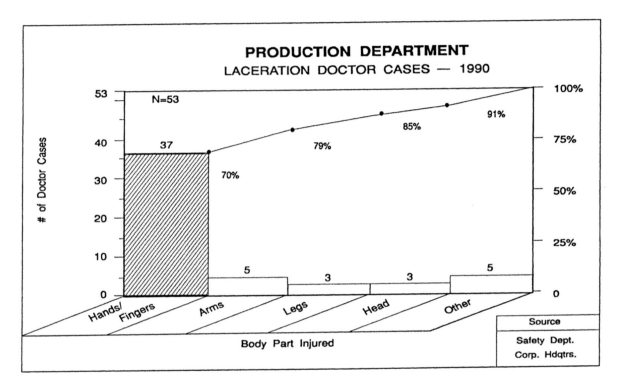

Figure 4-29

Next, the team agreed to the following interim target: *No more than 9 hand/finger related doctor cases in the Production Department by July 1991.* The team wanted to totally eliminate hand/finger related doctor cases, but felt it was sufficient that the target they selected represented a 50% improvement over this same period in 1990. Next, they began the second problem-solving step, *Analysis*.

To analyze the causes of hand/finger related doctor cases the team used CAUSE-AND-EFFECT-ANALYSIS. From this analysis, four potential root causes were identified:

1. Carelessness/attitude
2. Employees do not have gloves, or gloves are unsafe
3. Gloves not accessible
4. Improper use of equipment

CASE 5: Improving Employee Safety

Meetings 6 - 9

The team began the task of verifying each root cause. A summary of their findings is listed in the *MATRIX* in Figure 4-30.

ROOT CAUSE VERIFICATION MATRIX

Potential Root Cause	Verified?	Verification
1. Carelessness/ attitude	No	The team could not verify this potential root cause using data. It was the team's opinion that carelessness contributed to the problem, but that it was probably more a symptom than a cause.
2. Employees do not have gloves or gloves are unsafe	Yes	The team scheduled a meeting with the Production Department to *INTERVIEW* various employees and visually inspect the condition of their gloves. The findings from these interviews are documented in the *PIE CHART* in Figure 4-31.
3. Gloves not accessible	Yes	The team conducted a *SURVEY* of the 37 Production Department employees involved in doctor cases in 1990. The survey was used to determine where the employee's gloves were at the time they were injured. Findings from 32 survey respondents are shown in the PIE CHART in Figure 4-32.
4. Improper use of equipment	No	The team could not verify this potential root cause with data. As before, the team felt that improper equipment usage had contributed to the problem, but they couldn't prove it.

Figure 4-30

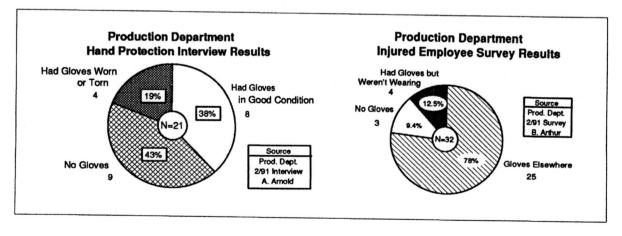

Figures 4-31 and 4-32

CASE 5: Improving Employee Safety

Two of the four potential root causes had been verified using data. Because both causes were closely related, the team agreed to address both of them in the next problem-solving step, *Evaluate Alternatives*.

Meetings 10 - 11

By using *BRAINSTORMING* and a *MATRIX*, two solutions were chosen and activities to accomplish them identified; see Figure 4-33.

ROOT CAUSE	SOLUTION	ACTIVITY TO ACCOMPLISH
Employees do not have gloves, or gloves are unsafe	Issue work gloves and reissue as needed	Add work gloves to storeroom inventory Storeroom to issue
Gloves not accessible	Issue glove clip (to hold gloves) to each employee	Purchase glove clips Storeroom to issue

Figure 4-33

The team performed a *BARRIERS & AIDS* analysis to help ensure that their solutions would be accepted. This analysis resulted in the addition of several activities to the detailed implementation plan shown in the *MATRIX* in Figure 4-34.

HAND/FINGER SAFETY IMPLEMENTATION PLAN				
What	**How**	**Who**	**When**	**Notes**
Research/ recommend work gloves and glove clips	Check with vendors Ensure that products are quality and price competitive Coordinate with purchasing supervisor	Tom Tom Tom	3/3/91 3/3/91 3/3/91	Complete Complete Complete
Develop procedure for issuing work gloves and clips	Develop procedures Ensure compatibility with existing procedures	Ken Ken	3/17/91 3/17/91	
Add work gloves and clips to storeroom inventory	Ensure space is available Add items to inventory control	Al Becky	3/17/91 3/17/91	
Storeroom to issue work gloves and glove clips	Get Mr. Steadman's approval	Team	3/24/91	
Communicate new procedure to affected employees	Draft safety bulletin from Mr. Steadman Discuss with union representative Include in safety procedures	Becky Al Ken	4/1/91 4/1/91 4/1/91	

Figure 4-34

CASE 5: Improving Employee Safety

Meetings 12 - 13

The team verified the details of their implementation plan, agreed that they were ready to present their findings to Mr. Steadman, and accepted assignments to prepare for the presentation.

Mr. Steadman was presented with the team's findings and enthusiastically agreed to test-implement them as soon as possible. The team began problem-solving step four, *Test-Implement*, and facilitated the implementation of their solutions for a three-month period. After this period, they met with Mr. Steadman again. At this presentation they used a *PARETO CHART* to communicate the effect of their actions; see Figure 4-35.

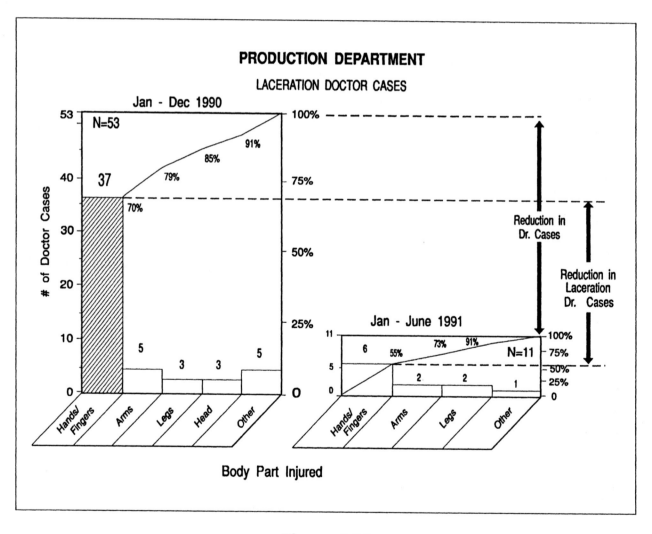

Figure 4-35

CASE 5: Improving Employee Safety

To *Standardize* their solutions, the team made the following recommendations:

- Include "Glove Safety" in the *Larry's Safety Handbook*
- Implement the same solutions in the Storage, Shipping, and Sales Departments
- Permit this team, or form another team, to investigate other causes of doctor cases (see Pareto chart in Figure 4-28).

THE QUALITY IMPROVEMENT STORY

Used in conjunction with the tools, the five problem-solving steps tell a *Quality Improvement (QI) Story* — a story of what a team or individual faced when they began, what they did, and the effect of their actions. A QI Story is a way of illustrating how the tools were applied and communicates to others the work of those who used the tools for quality improvement and problem solving steps.

A QI Story communicates with pictures more than words. The case studies you just read were similar to a QI Story, but such cases can sometimes be too narrative, too wordy. A QI Story sends a clear message without the assistance of a lot of words. Someone deserves credit for saying, "A picture is worth a thousand words." The QI Story is linked to that statement. After reviewing a QI Story, someone totally unfamiliar with the problem should be able to understand what was done and why, just by observing how the tools for quality improvement were applied.

Although all QI Stories are characterized by illustrations of the tools, they are different depending upon the problem being addressed, the tools used, and the team or individual that applied them. The constant among QI Stories is their use of the problem-solving steps. This "way of thinking" makes understanding the QI Story easier and ensures that a logical approach has been taken. An effective QI Story has several characteristics, as shown in Figure 4-36.

CHARACTERISTICS OF AN EFFECTIVE QI STORY

1. Interesting
2. Not too technical
3. Logically describes the actions taken
4. Uses tools correctly
5. Addresses a customer-related problem
6. Clearly shows improvement in the problem area selected

Figure 4-36

On the pages that follow, a QI Story is provided for case 5, "Improving Employee Safety." See for yourself whether this QI Story clearly communicates what was done, why, and the effect of the actions taken.

THE QI STORY

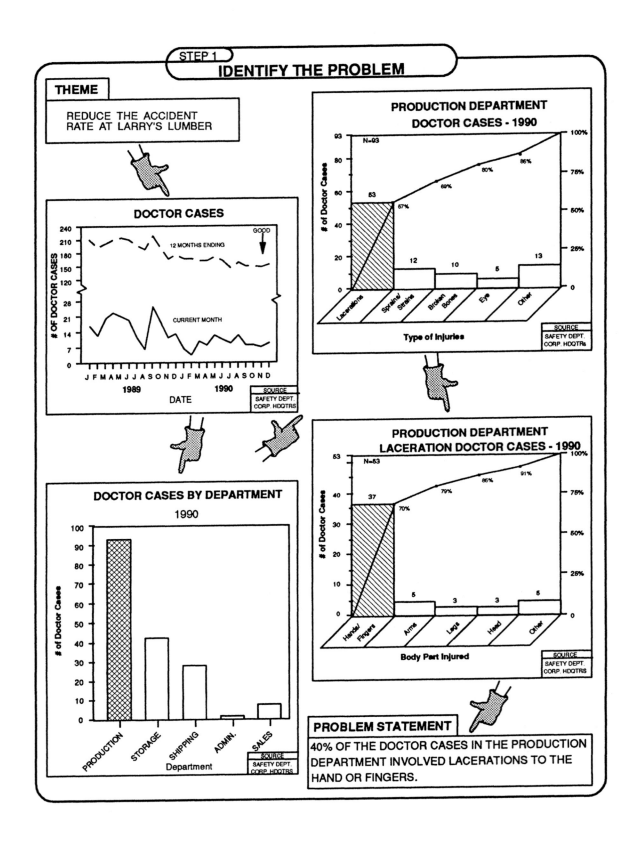

STEP 1

IDENTIFY THE PROBLEM

THEME

REDUCE THE ACCIDENT RATE AT LARRY'S LUMBER

DOCTOR CASES

(# OF DOCTOR CASES vs. DATE)

12 MONTHS ENDING
CURRENT MONTH
GOOD

J F M A M J J A S O N D J F M A M J J A S O N D
1989   1990
DATE

SOURCE
SAFETY DEPT.
CORP. HDQTRS

DOCTOR CASES BY DEPARTMENT

1990

(# of Doctor Cases by PRODUCTION, STORAGE, SHIPPING, ADMIN., SALES)

Department

SOURCE
SAFETY DEPT.
CORP. HDQTRS

PRODUCTION DEPARTMENT
DOCTOR CASES - 1990

N=93

53   57%
69%
80%
86%
100%

12   10   5   13

Lacerations Sprains/Strains Broken Bones Eye Other

Type of Injuries

SOURCE
SAFETY DEPT.
CORP. HDQTRs

PRODUCTION DEPARTMENT
LACERATION DOCTOR CASES - 1990

N=53

37   70%
79%
86%
91%
100%

5   3   3   5

Hands/Fingers Arms Legs Head Other

Body Part Injured

SOURCE
SAFETY DEPT.
CORP. HDQTRS

PROBLEM STATEMENT

40% OF THE DOCTOR CASES IN THE PRODUCTION DEPARTMENT INVOLVED LACERATIONS TO THE HAND OR FINGERS.

THE QI STORY

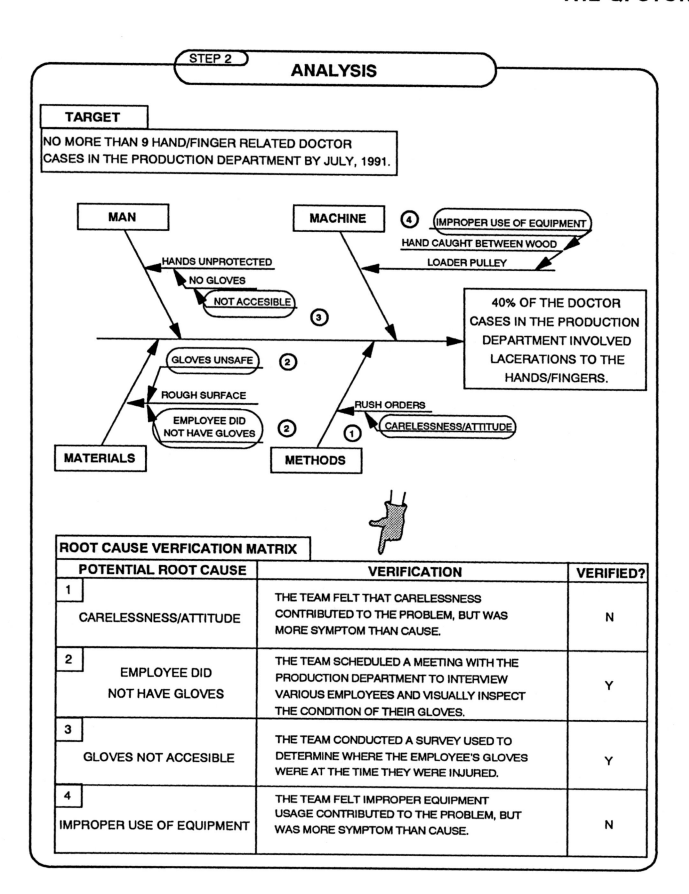

STEP 2   **ANALYSIS**

TARGET

NO MORE THAN 9 HAND/FINGER RELATED DOCTOR
CASES IN THE PRODUCTION DEPARTMENT BY JULY, 1991.

MAN

MACHINE

④ IMPROPER USE OF EQUIPMENT

HAND CAUGHT BETWEEN WOOD

LOADER PULLEY

HANDS UNPROTECTED

NO GLOVES

NOT ACCESIBLE

③

40% OF THE DOCTOR
CASES IN THE PRODUCTION
DEPARTMENT INVOLVED
LACERATIONS TO THE
HANDS/FINGERS.

GLOVES UNSAFE   ②

ROUGH SURFACE

EMPLOYEE DID
NOT HAVE GLOVES   ②

RUSH ORDERS

① CARELESSNESS/ATTITUDE

MATERIALS

METHODS

ROOT CAUSE VERFICATION MATRIX

POTENTIAL ROOT CAUSE	VERIFICATION	VERIFIED?
1 CARELESSNESS/ATTITUDE	THE TEAM FELT THAT CARELESSNESS CONTRIBUTED TO THE PROBLEM, BUT WAS MORE SYMPTOM THAN CAUSE.	N
2 EMPLOYEE DID NOT HAVE GLOVES	THE TEAM SCHEDULED A MEETING WITH THE PRODUCTION DEPARTMENT TO INTERVIEW VARIOUS EMPLOYEES AND VISUALLY INSPECT THE CONDITION OF THEIR GLOVES.	Y
3 GLOVES NOT ACCESIBLE	THE TEAM CONDUCTED A SURVEY USED TO DETERMINE WHERE THE EMPLOYEE'S GLOVES WERE AT THE TIME THEY WERE INJURED.	Y
4 IMPROPER USE OF EQUIPMENT	THE TEAM FELT IMPROPER EQUIPMENT USAGE CONTRIBUTED TO THE PROBLEM, BUT WAS MORE SYMPTOM THAN CAUSE.	N

THE QI STORY

STEP 3   **EVALUATE ALTERNATIVES**

ROOT CAUSE	SOLUTION	ACTIVITY TO ACCOMPLISH
Employees do not have gloves, or gloves are unsafe	Issue work gloves and reissue as needed	Add work gloves to storeroom inventory Storeroom to issue
Gloves not accesible	Issue glove clip (to hold gloves) to each employee	Purchase glove clips Storeroom to issue

BARRIERS	AIDS
Don't know what type of gloves/clips to purchase	Research and recommend gloves/clips
Some employees won't want to wear gloves	Develop procedures for gloves/clips
	Communicate procedure to employees

IMPLEMENTATION PLAN

WHAT	HOW	WHO	WHEN	NOTES
Research/recommend work gloves and clips	Check with vendors	Tom	3/3/91	Complete
	Ensure that products are quality and price competitive	Tom	3/3/91	Complete
	Coordinate with purchasing supervisor	Tom	3/3/91	Complete
Develop procedure for issuing work gloves and clips	Develop procedures	Ken	3/17/91	
	Ensure compatibility with existing procedures	Ken	3/17/91	
Add work gloves and clips to storeroom inventory	Ensure space is available	Al	3/17/91	
	Add items to inventory control	Becky	3/17/91	
Storeroom to issue work gloves and clips	Get Mr. Steadman's approval	Team	3/24/91	
Communicate new procedure to affected employees	Draft safety bulletin from Mr. Steadman	Becky	4/1/91	
	Discuss with union rep.	Al	4/1/91	
	Include in safety procedures	Ken	4/1/91	

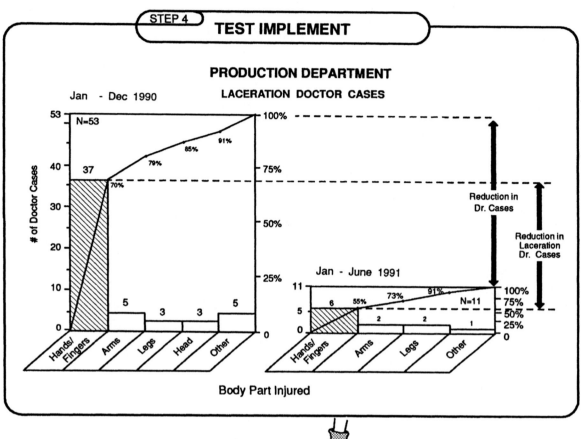

STEP 4   TEST IMPLEMENT

PRODUCTION DEPARTMENT
LACERATION DOCTOR CASES

Jan - Dec 1990

N=53

Body Part Injured

Jan - June 1991

Reduction in Dr. Cases

Reduction in Laceration Dr. Cases

STEP 5   STANDARDIZE

● INCLUDE GLOVE SAFETY PROCEDURES IN SAFETY HANDBOOK

● IMPLEMENT THE SAME SOLUTIONS IN STORAGE, SHIPPING AND SALES

● INVESTIGATE OTHER CAUSES OF DOCTOR CASES (SEE PARETO CHART, STEP 1)

THE QI STORY

IN CONCLUSION

Real quality is more than an expression. Quality is a condition embodied in a product or service shaped to meet the needs of its customer. Quality is possible only when products and services are continuously improved by applying the problem-solving steps and tools for quality improvement. Without this new way of thinking, the good products of today become the forgotten products of tomorrow, replaced by other products that have stayed in tune with customer needs.

The shift to something better is happening everywhere. New and better products abound. There are times when buying today doesn't make sense because anticipated improvements make waiting an intelligent alternative. Within organizations changes are rampant, too. Workers, departments, even machines that can't satisfy the customer who receives their output are in jeopardy. The prevailing attitude is, "If you can't do it, maybe an alternative is available that can."

The customer rules in this environment. And that's not bad, because you and I are also customers. It's when we put on our other hat, the one that says worker, that we must be aware of what the customer wants. We must satisfy the customer. To flourish in this environment, we must find out what the customer needs, plan to provide it in a form that meets those needs, and stay abreast of how we are doing, because customer needs change.

There are no shortcuts to quality. The tools you have read about in this book can help you build quality into your work and life. But these tools must be learned. Skill in applying them will only come from use. A surgeon or mechanic does not rely exclusively on the written word to become proficient with the tools of his or trade. A doctor learns to use a scalpel by working with it. A mechanic knows which tool to pull out of the tool kit, because he or she has spent many hours using the tools. By reading this book and becoming familiar with the tools for quality improvement, you have taken the first step. Begin mastering the tools by applying them every chance you get. There is no better way.

By themselves, the tools for quality improvement can help you communicate and understand. When used with the problem-solving steps, the tools become a powerful change agent that sends a clear message of why change is necessary and what must be done to achieve quality. Embedded in the problem-solving steps is a new way of thinking about what you do. The logic and order they provide give you confidence to approach your work from a new perspective. Instead of frustration, you are empowered to make a difference.

Having read this book, I hope that you are considering adopting a new way of thinking about what you do. I believe this shift is critical if work is to become meaningful and pride of craft is to return. We are all craftspeople; we produce something for others. But we are only as good as what we produce. To make work more than a paycheck, or a place to spend years performing a job like a machine, we must make something happen. Now you know how.

What makes each of us special is that we can think. This is a precious characteristic that should not be wasted. There are so many opportunities to use our minds to improve our lives. Experience alone cannot bring about the improvements that will lead to quality. You must have knowledge to make that experience beneficial. This book, however simple, has provided you with knowledge. Go now, and apply what you have read to make your life better in the days to come.

GLOSSARY

Analysis

Actions taken to identify the causes of a problem or condition, usually through the use of data.

Continuous Improvement

A four-phase cycle of ongoing positive change that encompasses:

1. *Planning* what is to be done
2. *Doing* what has been planned
3. *Checking* what has been done
4. *Acting* to prevent error or to improve

Criteria

Standards against which something can be judged or assessed.

Customer

The person or persons, either internal or external, who receive your products or services.

Data

Information or a set of facts presented in descriptive, or quantitative form.

Frequency

The number of times an event or value occurs in a given period.

Need

A condition expressed by customers (internal or external) that must be satisfied; an expression of something necessary, desired, or useful.

Output

The end result of a set of activities or work process.

Problem

A situation or condition in need of improvement.

Process

A set of activities (including people, materials, equipment, and methods) that combine to produce an output (product or service).

Process Control

Maintaining a desired state in the output of a process.

QI Story

Quality improvement story: a communication tool that illustrates how various tools and techniques have been applied to reduce or eliminate a problem.

QI Teams

People working together toward a common goal in quality improvement.

Range   The difference between the highest and lowest data points.

Reduction Problems   Problems in which improvement is possible, but elimination of the problem is unlikely.

Refined Number   The most specific or detailed number in a set of numbers.

Root Cause   The underlying reason for the occurrence of a problem.

Standardize   To take actions to ensure consistency.

Stratify   To break something down (data, a problem) into its component parts.

Symptom   An indication that a problem exists.

Systematic   Accomplishing a task according to a planned method or approach.

Target   A desired level of performance.

Teamwork   Working with others to accomplish a common goal or objective.

Variation   Differences in the output of process resulting from the influence(s) of people, machines (equipment), materials, and/or methods.

Zero Problems   Problems that can be totally eliminated.

BIBLIOGRAPHY

Amsden, Robert T., Howard E. Butler, and Davida M. Amsden. *SPC Simplified: Practical Steps to Quality.* White Plains, NY: Quality Resources, 1989.

Deming, W. Edwards. *Out of the Crisis.* Cambridge, MA: Massachusetts Institute of Technology, Center for Advanced Engineering Study, 1986.

Imai, Masaaki. *Kaizen: The Key to Japan's Competitive Success.* New York: Random House, 1986.

Ishikawa, Kaoru. *Guide to Quality Control.* 2nd rev. ed. Tokyo: Asian Productivity Organization, 1986; Quality Resources, distributor.

Ishikawa, Kaoru. *What is Total Quality Control? The Japanese Way.* Translated by David J. Lu. New York: Prentice Hall, 1985.

Juran, J. M. *Juran on Leadership for Quality.* New York: The Free Press, 1989.

Juran, J. M. *Juran on Planning for Quality.* New York: The Free Press, 1988.

Juran, J. M. *Juran's Quality Control Handbook.* 4th ed. New York: McGraw-Hill, 1988.

Kume, Hitoshi, ed. *Statistical Methods for Quality Improvement.* Tokyo: Association for Overseas Technical Scholarship (AOTS)/3A Corporation, 1985; Quality Resources, distributor.

Mizuno, Shigeru. *Company-wide Total Quality Control.* Tokyo: Asian Productivity Organization, 1988; Quality Resources, distributor.

Mizuno, Shigeru, ed. *Management for Quality Improvement: The 7 New QC Tools.* Cambridge, MA: Productivity Press, 1988.

Scherkenbach, William W. *The Deming Route to Quality and Productivity: Roadmaps and Roadblocks.* New York: Mercury Press/Fairchild Publications, 1990.

Shewhart, Walter A. *Statistical Method from the Viewpoint of Quality Control.* New York: Dover, 1986.

Walton, Mary. *The Deming Management Method.* New York: Perigee Books/Putnam Publishing Group, 1986.

INDEX

A

Accident rate. *See* Employee safety

Adjustment, 41

Aids. *See* Barriers & Aids

Alternatives, 22, 34-39, 150

    customer inquiries, 127
    employee safety, 144
    invoice processing, 135
    suggestion program, 120
    training effectiveness, 111

American quality, 14

Analysis, 12, 20, 22, 29-33, 149

    customer inquiries, 125
    employee safety, 142
    invoice processing, 132
    suggestion program, 118
    training effectiveness, 110

Automobile examples. *See* Car examples

B

Bar chart, 25, 33, 41, 49-52, 81, 101, 104

    employee safety, 140
    examples, 7, 26, 49, 140
    hints, 51-52
    instructions, 49-51
    types, 50

Barriers & Aids, 12, 53-55

    customer inquiries, 127

Barriers & Aids (*continued*)

    employee safety, 144
    examples, 37, 53, 113
    hints, 55
    instructions, 54
    invoice processing, 135
    suggestion program, 120
    training effectiveness, 113

Bars, histogram, 73-75

Bergamini, David, 20

Bimodal histogram, 77

Boundary lines, 73, 74

Brainstorming, 56-58

    barriers & aids, 54
    cause-and-effect diagram, 60, 61, 62
    customer inquiries, 123, 127
    employee safety, 144
    examples, 56
    hints, 58
    instructions, 56-57
    invoice processing, 135
    list reduction, 85, 86
    matrix, 87, 91
    problem-solving, 23, 31, 34, 43
    suggestion program, 118, 120
    teamwork, 18
    training effectiveness, 110, 111, 113
    types, 57

Broken tooth histogram, 77

C

Car examples, 5-9, 11-12, 88, 94, 96

Case studies, 106-46

customer inquiries, 123-30
employee safety, 138-46
invoice processing, 131-37
suggestion program, 117-22
training effectiveness, 109-16

Cause-and-effect analysis, 118, 142

see also Cause-and-effect diagram;
Root causes

Cause-and-effect diagram, 31-32,
59-65

examples, 32, 59, 119, 134
hints, 64-65
instructions, 60-64
invoice processing, 134-35
suggestion program, 118-19
see also Fishbone diagram

Change process, 9-10, 45

Charts and graphs, 25, 31, 33, 41

see also specific type, e.g., Bar chart

Checking errors, 12, 43

Checksheet, 9, 31, 33, 41, 66-68, 81,
104

customer inquiries, 124
examples, 25, 66
hints, 68
instructions, 66-68

Clustered bar chart, 50

Comb histogram, 77

Communication, 41

Confidentiality, 57

Consistency, 20

Continuous improvement, 44-45

Control chart, 48

Conversational interview, 80

Criteria, 87, 88, 89

Customer-related problems, 123-30

flowchart, 69-70
line graph, 82
problem-solving, 23-24, 29, 44
survey, 102

Cut-off histogram, 78

D

Data gathering, 12, 13, 19, 24-25

cause-and-effect diagram, 63
checksheet, 66-68
guidelines, 30-31
histogram, 73-76
interview, 81
line graph, 83

Data points, 73, 75, 76, 83

Deming, W. Edwards, 3, 4, 45

Diagrams. See Cause-and effect
diagram; Charts and graphs;
Fishbone diagram

E

Efficiency, 85

Employee safety, 138-46

Errors, 11, 12

Evaluation, 22, 34-39, 150

criteria, 88-89
customer inquiries, 127
employee safety, 144

Evaluation *(continued)*

    invoice processing, 135
    suggestion program, 120
    training effectiveness, 111

F

Family expenses examples, 92-97

Fifth-level causes, 63

Fire fighting, 44

First level causes, 61

Fishbone diagram, 59, 60-64, 118, 134

Flowchart, 31, 43, 44-45, 69-71

    customer inquiries, 125, 129, 137
    examples, 45, 69, 125, 129, 133
    hints, 71
    instructions, 70-71
    invoice processing, 132-33

Fourth-level causes, 63

Frequency measurement, 72, 75, 83, 94

G

Gains maintenence, 43

Glossary of terms, 155-56

Graphs. *See* Charts and graphs;
  specific type; e.g., Line graph

Grocery store examples, 10, 11

H

Histogram, 25, 33, 41, 72-78

    examples, 72, 116

Histogram *(continued)*

    hints, 76-78
    instructions, 73-76
    training effectiveness, 112, 114, 116
    types, 76-78

Horizontal axis, 83

I

Identification, 22, 23-28, 148

    customer inquiries, 123
    employee safety, 138-39
    suggestion program, 117-18
    training effectiveness, 109-10

Implementation, 22, 36-42, 53

    see also Test-implementation

Improvement opportunities. *See* Problem-solving; Quality improvement

Inefficiency, 69

Information gap, 2

Inquiring mind, 11

Instructor skill, 111

Interim target, 28, 36

Interview, 9, 23, 34, 79-81, 91, 103

    examples, 79
    hints, 81
    instructions, 79-81
    invoice processing, 135
    training effectiveness, 111

Invoice processing, 131-37

J

Japanese quality, 3, 14-15

Juran, Joseph, 97

K

Knowledge base, 12-13

L

Line graph, 25, 41, 52, 82-84
    customer inquiries, 124, 128
    employee safety, 138-39
    examples, 8, 19, 82, 115, 117, 122,
        124, 128, 132, 136, 139
    hints, 83-84
    instructions, 82-83
    invoice processing, 131-32, 135-36
    suggestion programs, 122
    training effectiveness, 111, 114-15

List reduction, 23, 85-86, 91
    customer inquiries, 123
    examples, 85
    hints, 86
    instructions, 86
    training effectiveness, 110, 113

Logic, 108

M

Machine problems, 53, 66-68

Management problems, 20

Manufacturing revenues, 98-99

Margenau, Henry, 20

Mathematics skills, 2-3, 10, 12-13

Matrix, 31, 35, 38, 86, 87-91
    customer inquiries, 123, 127
    employee safety, 143-44
    examples, 24, 87, 112, 121, 143, 144
    hints, 91
    instructions, 88-91
    suggestion programs, 120, 121
    training effectiveness, 112

Measurement
    line graph, 82-83
    training effectiveness, 109-16

Medical expenses examples, 96

Mistakes. *See* Errors

Monitoring, 41

Morale, 29

N

Normal histogram, 76

Numerical rating, 89

O

Objective questions, 80

Observation periods, 67

One-at-a-time brainstorming, 57, 110

Open door brainstorming, 57

Open-ended questions, 81, 104

Options, 87, 88, 89

Output, 4

Overtime, 33, 56

P

Pareto, Vilfredo, 97

Pareto chart, 25, 31, 41, 81, 92-97, 104
  customer inquiries, 126-27
  employee safety, 140-42, 145
  examples, 6, 7, 33, 92, 126, 141, 142, 145
  hints, 96-97
  instructions, 93-96

Pareto distribution, 97

Patience, 44

People
  interviewing, 79
  types of, 9

Percentage, 94-96, 99

Performance, 25, 28

Phone call examples. *See* Telephone call examples

Pie chart, 25, 41, 81, 98-101, 104
  examples, 98, 100, 133, 136, 143
  hints, 101
  instructions, 99-101
  invoice processing, 131-33, 135-36

Plan, do, check, and act, 70

Planning, 38

Point scoring, 89

Pre/post testing, 112

Problem-selection matrix, 87, 89, 90

Problem-solving, 18-45
  applications, 44-45

Problem-solving *(continued)*
  steps, 21-43, 108, 147
    alternatives, 34-39
    analysis, 29-33
    identification, 23-28
    linkage, 22
    standardization, 42-43
    test-implementation, 40-42
    see also specific step, e.g., Alternatives
  tools, 18-21
    see also specific tool, e.g., Bar chart

Problem statements, 26-27

Procedures, 43

Process, 4, 36, 69, 70

Q

Quality improvement
  applications, 106-46
    customer inquiries, 123-30
    employee safety, 138-46
    invoice processing, 131-37
    suggestion program, 117-22
    training effectiveness, 109-16
  benefits, 2-15
  problem-solving, 18-45
    see also Problem-solving
  tools, 4-5, 9-13, 18-21, 48-105
    bar chart, 49-52
    barriers & aids, 53-55
    brainstorming, 56-58
    cause-and-effect diagram, 59-65
    checksheet, 66-68
    flowchart, 69-71
    histogram, 72-78
    interview, 79-81
    line graph, 82-84
    list reduction, 85-86
    matrix, 87-91
    Pareto chart, 92-97

Quality improvement *(continued)*
    pie chart, 98-101
    QI story, 147-53
    survey, 102-5
    see also specific tool, e.g.,
    Bar chart

Quantity measurement, 83

Questionnaires. *See* Survey

R

Reduction problem, 34

Reinforcement, 41

Responsiblity, 43

Restaurant survey, 102-3

Root causes, 29-34
    cause-and-effect diagram, 59, 63, 64
    customer inquiries, 127
    employee safety, 142-44
    identification, 29-31, 33
    invoice processing, 135
    reduction, 34
    suggestion program, 120, 121
    verification, 31-32

Rules of order, 58

S

Safety. *See* Employee safety

Sales chart, 56, 57, 58

Scale, 90

Scientific Method, The (Margenau
  and Bergamini), 20-21

Scribe, 58

Second-level causes, 62, 96, 142

Size comparison, 98

Skewed histogram, 78

Solutions, 35-38, 40-43
    cause-and-effect diagram, 65
    invoice processing, 135

Spikes (graph), 84

Spotlight effect, 42

Standardization, 22, 42-43, 151
    customer inquiries, 129, 137
    employee safety, 146
    suggestion programs, 122
    training effectiveness, 116

Stratified bar chart, 50

Suggestion program case, 117-22

Survey, 6, 23, 34, 79, 91, 102-5
    examples, 102
    hints, 104-5
    instructions, 103-4
    suggestion program, 118
    training effectiveness, 111, 114

Symbols, flowchart, 71

Symptoms, problem, 29

Systematic approach. *See*
  Problem-solving

T

Target setting, 28, 36

Teamwork, 12, 13, 18, 29, 131

Telephone call examples, 69-71, 72-78

Test-implementation, 22, 40-42, 151
    cause-and-effect diagram, 65
    customer inquiries, 128
    employee safety, 145
    invoice processing, 137
    training effectiveness, 112, 114, 116

Thinking problems, 2-15, 108

Third-level causes, 62

Time-based measurements, 52, 83

Training effectiveness case, 109-16

Trial and error, 11

True/false questions, 80, 81

Typing errors examples, 65

V

Variation, 4

Vertical axis, 83

Voting, 85, 86

W

Wedge, 99

Work activities, 43

Work teams. *See* Teamwork

Write-it-down brainstorming, 57

XYZ

X-axis, 83

Y-axis, 83

Zero problem, 34

Printed in the United States
28790LVS00001B/3-82

9 780527 916527